Funding International Arbitration

Editors
Sherina Petit and Nosherwan Vakil

Managing director
Sian O'Neill

Funding International Arbitration
is published by

Globe Law and Business Ltd
3 Mylor Close
Horsell
Woking
Surrey GU21 4DD
United Kingdom
Tel: +44 20 3745 4770
www.globelawandbusiness.com

Printed and bound by 4Edge Ltd, Hockley, Essex

Funding International Arbitration

ISBN 9781837230211
EPUB ISBN 9781837230228
Adobe PDF ISBN 9781837230235

Table of contents

Introduction

Sherina Petit
Stewarts
Nosherwan Vakil
The 36 Group

The genesis of *Funding International Arbitration* can be traced back to a significant turning point in our work, when we were confronted with a number of queries from clients from across the world about the options for funding disputes. When we reviewed the information available, we noticed a dearth of practical guidance on funding which explained it in plain and simple language for the commercial individual to understand. We therefore began to develop a comprehensive yet accessible guide to demystify the concept of funding, providing real examples, insights and strategies.

Each chapter of this Special Report is written by individuals who deal with funding day in, day out – funders, brokers and practitioners. The Special Report encourages the reader to consider whether funding is appropriate for their dispute by providing guidance on the funding process from initial assessment to enforcement. In this regard, the Special Report's structure is meticulously designed to provide an overview of the funding process, including funding options, pre-funding considerations, market regulation, legal barriers to funding, cost management, enforcement mechanisms and dispute avoidance strategies. The chapters within provide strategies along with a holistic perspective of the funding landscape, allowing the reader to make well-informed decisions.

At the heart of this Special Report is a deep commitment to fostering an environment that maximises the potential of funding in international arbitration and promotes innovation and accessibility in dispute resolution. We hope that the information and insights in this Special Report on approaching funders, managing ongoing relationships with funders and optimising financial positions will enable practitioners, funders and clients to navigate the funding landscape with confidence and precision.

In the context of the contemporary international arbitration funding regime, one critical impediment faced is the lack of awareness about the role and mechanics of funding, as well as misconceptions about funding. Furthermore, the evolving regulatory landscape governing arbitration funding adds a layer of complexity necessitating careful planning and expertise.

In this dynamic environment, both funders and clients encounter the inherent risks of funding. Funders must carefully assess the merits and risks of the potential cases to make informed investment decisions; while users must weigh the potential benefits of funding against the associated costs and obligations. Balancing these considerations and effectively managing risk is critical to the success of funded arbitration proceedings.

Recognising these pressing concerns, this Special Report emerges as a timely response to tackling current challenges, providing invaluable insights and dispelling misconceptions pertaining to funding.

As we navigate the ever-evolving landscape of international arbitration, we are confident that *Funding International Arbitration* will serve as a reliable companion, guiding practitioners, clients and funders to success.

At the outset of this transformative journey, we invite practitioners and stakeholders alike to join us in exploring the rapidly evolving landscape of arbitration funding and charting breakthroughs in the pursuit of equity.

I. The growth of the funding market in the UK and beyond

Stavros Brekoulakis
National University of Singapore; 3 Verulam Buildings
Julian DM Lew KC
Twenty Essex; Queen Mary University of London
Simona Valkova
Independent tribunal secretary

1. History and development of third-party funding

Traditionally, in most jurisdictions, there was no right to fund, take over or share in the success (and risk) of someone else's litigation. Such arrangements were either considered illegal under the doctrines of maintenance and champerty (in common law jurisdictions) or declared a criminal offence or a civil tort.[1] One of the main reasons for this prohibition was because the funder would often use the financial help provided as leverage for its own interests.[2]

However, in recognition of the greater access to justice that third-party funding affords, things have slowly changed. Today, many jurisdictions have revisited their prohibitions and/or restrictions on third-party funding.

In May 2023, the Nigerian Arbitration and Mediation Act 2023 came into force and repealed the (old) Arbitration and Conciliation Act 1988.[3] The 2023 act expressly abolishes the application of the torts of champerty and maintenance to third-party funding in arbitrations seated in Nigeria.[4] Section 62 requires parties to disclose the name and address of any third-party funder before and during arbitral proceedings. Section 62(3) provides that if a respondent makes a security for costs application based on a third-party funding disclosure, the "tribunal may allow the funded party or its counsel to provide an affidavit" confirming whether "the funder has agreed to cover adverse costs orders", which will be a "relevant consideration to the tribunal's decision on whether to grant security for costs".[5]

In Ireland, maintenance and champerty have been criminal offences and civil torts since the 1600s. In May 2017, the Irish Supreme Court reaffirmed this prohibition, holding (by a clear majority of four to one) that a third-party funding agreement between a claimant and an English third-party funder violated the laws on maintenance and champerty under ancient statutes from the 14th century to the Maintenance and Embracery Act 1634.[6] However, having reaffirmed the common law prohibition of third-party funding, a number of Supreme Court judges expressed their disquiet over some important implications emanating from this prohibition, observing that "it is at least arguable that there is a very real problem in practice about access to justice [which] is growing".[7] While acknowledging the reasons for his colleagues' decision, Justice McKechnie further observed that:

> *the conclusions so reached represents a deeply unsatisfactory outcome ... The outcome of this case is manifestly troublesome from the perspective of the giving of effect to the constitutional right of access to the courts; indeed, all the more so given the importance of the questions at issue.*

Importantly, too, the judges invited the Irish legislature to act upon and regulate third-party funding in the future to address the conflicting considerations underpinning the doctrine of maintenance on the one hand and the right of access to justice on the other.[8]

The Irish legislature answered this call of the Supreme Court, with the Department of Justice confirming that the restriction on third-party funding would be removed through a government amendment to the Courts and Civil Law (Miscellaneous Provisions) Bill.[9] Consequently, on 5 July 2023, the Courts and Civil Law (Miscellaneous Provisions) Act 2023 was signed into law.[10] Notably, the new act contains a section which specifically refers to the Arbitration Act 2010 and states that "the offences and torts of maintenance and champerty do not apply to dispute resolution proceedings".[11] It further provides that the use of third-party funding contracts in dispute resolution proceedings will not be treated as contrary to "public policy or otherwise illegal or void" as long as it meets the criteria provided for in the law.[12]

Following this development, on 17 July 2023, the Law Reform Commission of Ireland published a consultation paper on third-party funding in litigation in recognition of the fact that the "policy and legal context for third-party funding has shifted considerably".[13] It remains to be seen what further changes might be introduced following publication of the Law Reform Commission's report.

Other common law jurisdictions have already introduced reforms expressly permitting third-party funding in international arbitration. Notably, Singapore and Hong Kong enacted legislative reforms to permit third-party funding arrangements that were previously prohibited. The new legislation expressly provides that the doctrines of maintenance and champerty do not apply to domestic or international arbitration.[14] The proposed amendments also establish certain disclosure obligations for funded parties, as well as ethical and other standards for counsel and third-party funders.

In particular, in 2017, Singapore amended its law to permit third-party funding in relation to prescribed dispute resolution proceedings under certain conditions.[15] Specifically, a number of qualifications for funders were set out, including requirements that the funder:

- cover the cost of the proceedings to which it is not a party;[16] and
- have "a paid-up share capital of not less than S$5 million or the equivalent amount in foreign currency or not less than S$5 million or the equivalent amount in foreign currency in managed assets".[17]

Other common law jurisdictions have already introduced reforms expressly permitting third-party funding in international arbitration. Notably, Singapore and Hong Kong enacted legislative reforms to permit third-party funding arrangements that were previously prohibited.

In June 2017, Hong Kong enacted the Arbitration and Mediation Legislation (Third-Party Funding) Ordinance 2017 (Amendment Ordinance), which expressly permits third-party funding arrangements.[18] More recently, in February 2019, the government published the Code of Practice for Third-Party Funders, which was foreshadowed in the 2017 legislation.[19] The code is a significant regulatory instrument, setting out standards and practices which third-party funders must observe in order to operate in the Hong Kong arbitration market. These standards include requirements that a funder maintain:

- access to minimum capital of HK$20 million; and
- the capacity to:
  - "pay all debts when they become due and payable"; and
  - "cover all of its aggregate funding liabilities under all of its funding agreements for a minimum period of 36 months".[20]

The code further prohibits a funder from influencing in any way the funded party or its legal representative or taking control of the conduct of the arbitration, "except to the extent permitted by law".[21]

In 2017, the High Level Committee in India presented a report on its review of "the institutionalisation of arbitration mechanism in India" to the government of India. The report made several recommendations to promote arbitration in India, giving as an example the adoption of favourable third-party funding legislation.[22] Following this, in May 2023, the New Delhi High Court issued a judgment recognising the validity of third-party funding in India. The court also held that although transparency is desirable when it comes to disclosing the use of third-party funding in an arbitration, this is "a relevant fact" when determining an order for security for costs: "permitting enforcement of an arbitral award against a non-party which has not accepted any such risk, is neither desirable nor permissible."[23]

In England and Wales, maintenance and champerty have not constituted criminal offences or civil torts since the introduction of the Criminal Law Act 1967. However, no formal regulation on third-party funding has been passed either. Instead, it used to be subject to self-regulation in the form of a voluntary Code of Conduct for Litigation Funders which was adopted in January 2014 by the Association of Litigation Funders. However, since the code was amended in 2018, it no longer applies to third-party arbitration funding; rather it applies only to litigation funding.[24] Thus, third-party funding in arbitration remains effectively unregulated in England and Wales.

Other jurisdictions have more recently enacted legislation on third-party funding. For example, the chief justice of the Abu Dhabi Global

Market Courts prescribed the Litigation Funding Rules 2019 in April 2019.[25] The rules require funders:

- "to carry on as a principal business the funding of proceedings to which the funder is not a party";
- to have qualifying assets of not less than $5 million or the equivalent amount in foreign currency; and
- not to be owned, "(whether wholly or partly, and whether directly or indirectly, and whether by way of shares or otherwise) by a lawyer or a law firm: (i) who has introduced or referred the funder to a client in relation to the proceedings; or (ii) whose client has a Litigation Funding Agreement in force with the funder in relation to ongoing proceedings".[26]

Australia has also recently amended its legislation. After abolishing the criminalisation of maintenance and champerty (in most part) and declaring that third-party funding is not contrary to public policy or an abuse of process,[27] Australia enacted the Corporations Amendment (Litigation Funding) Regulations 2020, which came into effect on 24 July 2020. The regulations aim to increase the accountability of funders operating in Australia and to improve transparency.[28] Thus, since July 2020, litigation funders in Australia are "required to hold an Australian Financial Services License (AFSL) and comply with the managed investment scheme regime (MIS)".[29] Unfortunately, no mention of arbitration is made.

The European Commission is also looking to impose restrictions on third-party funding. In September 2022, the European Parliament passed a resolution with recommendations to the commission and a request for the promulgation of a directive "to establish common minimum standards at Union level on commercial third party litigation funding".[30] The European Parliament appended a draft directive to its resolution addressing a range of legal and financial issues related to both the terms of third-party funding agreements and the management of corporations involved in third-party funding in Europe.[31] Specifically, it proposes:

- a potential cap of 40% on the share of recovery for funders;
- an obligation to pay adverse costs and for the mandatory disclosure of funding agreements;
- the introduction of an authorisation system for litigation funders; and
- new requirements for financial adequacy.

The adoption of the draft directive has been delayed following criticism from the International Legal Finance Association (ILFA) that the proposed rules were based on a "lack of evidence" and would "undermine the availability of legal finance in the EU".[32] Some of the recommendations made by the ILFA include that the European Union should consult "with key consumer rights groups, the European Innovation Council and [the] SMEs Executive Agency on the impact of curbing legal finance on emerging technologies and breakthrough innovations" before considering any further legislation on legal finance.[33] It has been further reported that the European Commission now plans to conduct "a mapping study of the existing European funding landscape" before introducing any new rules.[34]

It is unclear whether the draft directive will eventually be passed and if so, when; however, one can assume that some form of regulation will be introduced at the EU level, as there appears to be a growing consensus within the European Union that soft law approaches and self-regulation of third-party funding have not been effective.

2. What is 'third-party funding'?

Any effort to regulate requires a clear definition of the object to be regulated. However, a precise definition of 'third-party funding' remains elusive. Funders themselves disagree over this, with some arguing that it is incapable of definition.[35]

Third-party funding is difficult to define because various forms of financing claims and paying for legal costs have long existed which are similar to, or which definitionally overlap with, modern forms of third-party funding. In some jurisdictions, contingency fee arrangements (CFAs) facilitate legal representation and/or cover claimants' expenses. Although rarely referenced explicitly as a form of third-party funding, law firms are non-parties that advance costs and waive the cost of fees contingent on the outcome of a case.[36] Equally, modern third-party funding can be functionally similar to, serve purposes similar to and operate as a market alternative for before-the-event (BTE), after-the-event (ATE) or traditional liability insurance. Some third-party funders provide products that are effectively a form of ATE insurance; and ATE insurance is often purchased contemporaneously on entering into a third-party funding agreement.

Third-party funding is also difficult to define because of the wide range of funding models that already exist and the rapid evolution and introduction of new models, including some designed to evade a definition. Funding may be structured:

- through corporate debt or equity;
- as risk-avoidance instruments or full transfers of the underlying claims; or
- through special purpose vehicles (SPVs).[37]

Any effort to regulate requires a clear definition of the object to be regulated. However, a precise definition of 'third-party funding' remains elusive.

Equity investing by third-party funders is also increasingly common. Under this mode, a funder purchases shares of a company (often one that is in financial distress) and then assumes seats on its board. In that context, the funder (or its SPV) will be directly providing funding as an owner/shareholder. Under this scenario, neither the party nor the shareholder receives funding from an outside source, which makes most traditional definitions inapplicable and may raise practical questions about the identity of the funder and the application of particular rules to a funder.[38]

More recently, law firm financing and portfolio funding have emerged as new models to fund an identified range of cases involving a particular party or law firm. In the latter instance, funding is provided to the law firm, not the party, which can raise additional practical and definitional challenges. An additional complexity is that one portfolio of cases can be identified to receive funding while another is the basis for a funder's return or securitisation of its investment. In that case, funding may be provided for one case, but the funder may have no interest in the actual outcome of that particular case. More recently, funded cases and particularly portfolios of funded cases can be 'refinanced', meaning that a second third-party funder (or multiple other investors) can invest in a portfolio or a 'bundle' of cases of another funder.

Third-party funders may become involved either before a claim is filed or later in the process.[39] Some funders specialise only in award execution or funding for expert witness costs; while others fund all costs, including a potential adverse award of costs. These distinctions raise questions about the potential enforcement of any regulations imposed on funders, which must necessarily impose an ongoing duty to be effective.

While most funders invest in claims, it is also possible to invest in the respondent's defence or counterclaim. In such cases, the funder's interest is usually tied to the political and policy implications (not financial) of the award. For example, in the investment arbitration brought by Philip Morris against Uruguay, the Bloomberg Foundation and its Campaign for Tobacco-Free Kids provided outside financial support for the Uruguayan government.[40] Other types of respondent-side funding, more functionally similar to ATE insurance, have been discussed, but the general consensus is that such funding models are at best occasional and perhaps only hypothetical.

Respondent states can also be funded by another state or, as has been reported anecdotally by some funders, have their costs for defence or for counterclaims funded through a model similar to ATE insurance. There has also been at least one case in which a respondent state was funded by an oil company that had a competing claim to the oil rights being sought by the investor in the funded case.[41] Given the use of precedent in investor-state dispute settlement, it is plausible that funders, as 'repeat players', may 'play for the rules' and intentionally select so-called 'test cases' to establish precedent.

In the past, some arbitral institutions have also attempted to provide a definition of 'third-party funding', if only for the purposes of their respective rules and the obligation that some of them impose on parties to disclose the existence of third-party funding and the identity of the funder. For instance, the 2017 China International Economic and Trade Arbitration Commission (CIETAC) Rules define 'third-party funding' as:

> *the situation where a natural person or an entity, who is not a party to the dispute, provides funds to a party to the arbitration to cover all or part of that party's costs for the arbitral proceedings, through an agreement with the party accepting the funding.*[42]

The Arbitration Foundation of South Africa International Arbitration Rules, amended in 2021, provide in Article 27(1) that a 'third-party funder' refers to:

> *any natural or legal person who is not a party to the arbitration and is not a Party Representative, but who enters into an agreement either with a party, an affiliate of that party, or a Party Representative in order to provide material or financial support for all or part of the cost of the arbitration, where such support is provided through a donation, or grant, or in exchange for remuneration or reimbursement wholly or partially dependent on the outcome of the arbitration.*

A 'third-party funding agreement' is defined as "an agreement by a party or potential party to the arbitration with a third-party funder for the funding of the arbitration".

Interestingly, while the 2021 International Chamber of Commerce (ICC) Rules do not define the terms 'third-party funding agreement' or 'third-party funder', they explicitly state in the Note to Parties and Arbitrators that, subject to any contrary determination by the tribunal in the specific case, the obligation to disclose a third-party funding agreement (if there is one) as well as the identity of the funder:

> *would normally not capture (i) inter-company funding within a group of companies, (ii) fee arrangements between a party and its counsel, or (iii) an indirect interest, such as that of a bank having*

A 'third-party funding agreement' is defined as "an agreement by a party or potential party to the arbitration with a third-party funder for the funding of the arbitration".

granted a loan to the party in the ordinary course of its ongoing activities rather than specifically for the funding of the arbitration.[43]

In contrast, in the 2022 International Centre for Settlement of Investment Disputes (ICSID) Arbitration Rules, 'third-party funding' is referred to as "a donation or grant, or in return for remuneration dependent on the outcome of the proceeding".[44]

Consequently, the challenges in developing a complete definition are significant, but necessary. The nature of policy concerns may shift considerably depending on the funding models. Similarly, the extent and nature of the definition may change depending on the regulatory context. The definition adopted as a target of disclosure obligations for the purpose of identifying potential arbitrator conflicts of interest may differ from the definition adopted for the purpose of prohibiting funding.

3. The growth of the third-party funding market

Litigation funding primarily emerged in the 1990s. In some countries, this followed the relaxation or complete removal of funding prohibitions and restrictions; while in others, this was considered a

Litigation funding primarily emerged in the 1990s. In some countries, this followed the relaxation or complete removal of funding prohibitions and restrictions; while in others, this was considered a new innovation.

new innovation. For instance, in Germany, commercial litigation funding was 'invented' by Foris AG in 1998.[45] In the Netherlands, Omni Bridgeway has been managing or funding litigation claims since 1986.[46] In Australia, the rise of litigation funding was driven by the introduction of legislation on class action disputes in 1992;[47] today, most major class actions in Australia are funded by private litigation finance companies.[48]

Litigation funding emerged in the United Kingdom following the introduction of two significant statutes. After the Criminal Law Act of 1967 decriminalised maintenance and champerty, as stated above:

- the Courts and Legal Services Act 1990[49] made CFAs legal in the United Kingdom; and
- the Access to Justice Act 1999[50] provided additional litigation funding means as an alternative to CFAs.[51]

This was reaffirmed by several Court of Appeal decisions between 2002 and 2005 which determined that third-party funding would not offend maintenance and champerty rules, if provided properly.[52]

However, a 2023 decision of the UK Supreme Court is regarded as a setback for litigation finance in England and Wales.[53] In essence, the court equated litigation finance agreements (under which a funder can recover part of the damages received) to 'damages-based agreements' (DBAs) within the meaning of Section 58AA(3) of the Courts and Legal Services Act 1990. The effect is that DBAs are now considered unenforceable under the current law, unless certain conditions are complied with.[54] This also applies to litigation finance agreements, to the extent that they do not comply with the act. The court recognised the significance of this decision by stating that: "the likely consequence in practice would be that most third-party litigation funding agreements would by virtue of [Section 58AA(3) of the Courts and Legal Services Act 1990] be unenforceable as the law currently stands."[55] It remains to be seen whether legislation will be introduced in the near future to reverse or confirm the effect of this judgment.

In contrast, the funding of international arbitration disputes is a comparatively new phenomenon, which began to emerge in 2008.[56] Since then, it has grown into a billion-dollar industry.[57] In 2020, FTI Consulting forecast that the global litigation funding investment market would reach $13 billion by 2021, with London cementing its position as the "global centre of this trend": reportedly, "£2 billion of cash [was] held by UK's litigation funders at the start of the year".[58] In 2022, it was reported that:

- the assets of UK litigation funders had "hit a record £2.2 billion last year, an 11% increase on the previous year";[59] and
- third-party funding had become "a global industry worth an estimated €40–€80 billion".[60]

The growth of third-party funding in international arbitration has been influenced by several factors, including:

- the benefits that third-party funding offers;
- parties' perceptions and attitudes towards the use of third-party funding in international arbitration, as well as their actual experience of using it;
- legislative changes over the past decade which have not only allowed for the use of third-party funding but also started regulating it (to varied extents); and
- uncertainties in the global markets.

Dispute funding facilitates access to justice because it allows parties, which would otherwise be unable to initiate or maintain a meritorious claim, to engage in the dispute resolution process. It also allows parties to share the risk and costs of funding the dispute (even where they can afford them), which:

- relieves cash-flow pressure;
- minimises the risk in case the claim is unsuccessful;[61] and
- in some cases, removes the undue advantage that the other party may have simply by being more affluent.

This is especially important in international arbitration, where the costs of some commercial and most investment disputes can be high, depending on:

- the complexity and size of the case;
- the duration of the process;
- the number of lawyers and arbitrators involved; and
- whether it is institutional or *ad hoc*.

Further, funders are usually only interested in good claims. In deciding whether to invest in a claim, they conduct thorough due diligence and an objective analysis of the party's case, which has several benefits:

- It can filter out unmeritorious claims;
- It can assist the party in shaping a strategy; and
- It can be used to encourage settlement of the dispute.

Another factor which has contributed to the growth of third-party funding is the change in parties' perceptions towards the use of third-

Dispute funding facilitates access to justice because it allows parties, which would otherwise be unable to initiate or maintain a meritorious claim, to engage in the dispute resolution process.

party funding in international arbitration.[62] In 2013, it was reported that the use of third-party funding and BTE insurance was relatively uncommon – respectively, just 6% and 20% of participating organisations availed of these options to fund disputes.[63] However, this began to change rapidly: in 2015, a Queen Mary-White & Case survey reported that when asked how familiar respondents were with the use of third-party funding in international arbitration:

- 39% had encountered it in practice;
- 12% had used it themselves; and
- 27% had seen it used.[64]

The survey concluded that the use of third-party funding had become "relatively widespread compared to" that of insurance products.[65] Further, when asked to rate their perceptions of third-party funding:

- 46% had a "neutral" perception;
- 28% had a "positive" perception; and
- 26% had a "negative" perception.

Notably, however:

- 51% of respondents who had used third-party funding reported a "positive" experience with it;

- 31% took a "neutral" view; and
- only 18% had a "negative" experience.[66]

By 2018, awareness of the use of third-party funding in international arbitration had increased further, with 42% of respondents to that year's survey having encountered it in practice either by using it themselves (16%) or by seeing it used (26%).[67] Further, the survey revealed a "clear shift from neutral to positive" perceptions since 2015. In particular:

- one-third of respondents expressed "neutral" perceptions;
- more than one-half of respondents indicated "positive" perceptions; and
- only 13% expressed "negative" perceptions.[68]

Interestingly, 75% of the respondents who had actually used third-party funding in practice reported a "positive" experience with it.[69] This data suggests that "the more users encounter third-party funding in practice, the more favourably they tend to perceive it".[70] Therefore, it is perhaps unsurprising that in 2021, 8% of survey respondents said that one of the factors that would make jurisdictions more attractive to users as seats of arbitration would be if they allowed for third-party funding (non-recourse).[71]

In recognition of these positive changes and the increased use of third-party funding in international arbitration, many legislative changes have taken place in the past five to six years. In addition to countries amending their domestic laws to provide specifically for third-party funding and regulate its use (as outlined above), a number of international arbitration institutions have done the same by amending their arbitration rules. For instance, the first arbitration rules to include provisions on third-party funding were the Singapore International Arbitration Centre (SIAC) Rules and the CIETAC Investment Arbitration Rules in 2017. The SIAC Rules empower the tribunal to order the disclosure of:

- the existence of a third-party funding agreement; and
- "the identity of the third-party funder and, where appropriate, details of the third-party funder's interest in the outcome of the proceedings, and/or whether or not the third-party funder has committed to undertake adverse costs liability".[72]

Similarly, the CIETAC Investment Arbitration Rules impose a direct obligation on the parties to inform the tribunal, the other party and the institution administering the case in writing of the existence of any third-party funding agreement.[73] In 2018, the Hong Kong International Arbitration Centre also amended its Arbitration Rules to impose a similar obligation upon the parties to disclose the "existence of any funding agreement", including the identity of any third-party funder.[74]

This approach was also followed in the Vienna International Arbitration Rules (as amended in 2021),[75] the International Chamber of Commerce Arbitration Rules[76] and the Arbitration Foundation of Southern Africa International Arbitration Rules.[77] More recently, ICSID published its amended Arbitration Rules in 2022 to introduce a provision on third-party funding. In particular, Article 14(1) requires parties to file "written notice disclosing the name and address of any non-party from which the party, directly or indirectly, has received funds for the pursuit or defense of the proceeding".[78]

Another key factor that has fostered the growth of third-party funding internationally is the ongoing economic uncertainty that continues to haunt the world markets, initially created by the 2008 global financial crisis and exacerbated by other economic disruptions such as COVID-19 and armed conflicts in different parts of the world.[79] Naturally, these economic constraints have had a negative impact on most companies and large corporate entities around the world. Corporations have been put in the tricky position of trying to respond with solidarity to the fallout from the COVID-19 pandemic while at the same time protecting shareholder value.[80]

According to a 2021 EY study, since the start of the pandemic, "32% of corporates had deferred or stopped the investigation of potential legal claims they would ordinarily have pursued, with 30% of corporates citing lack of funds as the reason for such deferrals".[81] Thus, it appears that demand for third-party funding is set to increase, since these businesses may now look to external funders to help them bring these claims.[82] This is not least because "liquidity management continues to be a central focus in companies' strategies for resilience" – initially against the pandemic[83] and more recently against rising interest rates, inflation and the impending withdrawal of government stimulus programmes. Third-party funding is seen as "a key tool" in managing liquidity because it helps to free up "working capital, taking costs liability off the balance sheet".[84] In fact, third-party funding is increasingly perceived as a "commercially prudent risk management tool for sophisticated businesses".[85]

4. Moral and ethical considerations

Potential arbitrator conflicts of interest were among the first and most prominent issues to attract attention in relation to third-party funders' participation in international arbitration. More specifically, questions have arisen as to whether, how, to what extent and by whom disclosures should be made to allow arbitrators, parties and institutions to assess potential conflicts of interest involving funders. These concerns were mainly due to several factors, including:

- arbitrators taking positions within, or playing *ad hoc* consultant roles for, some funders;
- the increasing number of cases involving third-party funding;
- the highly concentrated segment of the funding industry that invests in investment arbitration;
- the symbiotic relationship between funders and a small group of law firms; and
- related links between elite law firms and some leading arbitrators.

It had been argued that third-party funding should not cause potential conflicts of interest because it is simply one of many possible forms of financial support for pursuing or defending a dispute. The source of financing for a dispute is irrelevant to the merits of the dispute and consequently there is no reason to treat third-party funding as subject to any special treatment that would not apply, for example, to a corporate loan taken out for the purpose of pursuing a claim.

Some funders contend that the reason for opposing the disclosure of third-party funding is not to keep secret their presence or identity, but rather a reaction to perceived procedural and strategic consequences

It had been argued that third-party funding should not cause potential conflicts of interest because it is simply one of many possible forms of financial support for pursuing or defending a dispute.

of disclosure, such as allegedly frivolous challenges to arbitrators and unfounded requests for security for costs. Some also suggest that these responses to disclosure may not simply be a matter of case strategy, but rather an intentional effort to drive up the cost of a case to make the funding model untenable.

It has also been argued – and supported by some courts – that unknown conflicts of interest cannot be a basis for an effective challenge to an arbitrator or an award, or for a refusal to enforce an award. Although a resulting award may not always be subject to set-aside proceedings or refused enforcement, there are other potential costs to undisclosed conflicts, such as:

- wasted time and money;
- an arbitrator suffering the embarrassment of a public challenge to their integrity; or
- even the potential impact on the integrity and legitimacy of international arbitration itself.

It is for these reasons that legal frameworks and practices regarding arbitrator conflicts are based not on a 'see no evil' model, but instead on an affirmative duty for arbitrators to investigate potential conflicts.

Today, the prevailing consensus is that the existence of third-party funding can raise potential conflicts of interest for arbitrators and the existence of such arrangements as well as the identity of the funders should thus be disclosed. Potential arbitrator conflicts of interest are governed by numerous sources, including arbitral rules and national law, as explained above.

However, given that modern third-party funding is a relatively recent phenomenon, many of these sources have not yet specifically addressed the issue of potential conflicts of interest involving third-party funding. The International Bar Association (IBA) was the first body to formally address issues relating to third-party funding conflicts. The 2014 IBA Guidelines on Conflicts of Interest in International Arbitration provide that a party should disclose to the tribunal, the other party and the appointing institution "any relationship, direct or indirect":

- between one of the tribunal members and a party; or
- between an arbitrator and "any third person or entity with a direct economic interest" in the award to be rendered.[86]

This definition, however, still leaves some unresolved questions regarding the scope and application of the guidelines to certain types of dispute financing.

The 2017 Hong Kong Code of Practice for Third-Party Funders[87] also sets outs clear provisions on conflicts of interest. It requires funders to "maintain, for the duration of the funding agreement, effective procedures for managing any conflict of interest that may arise". These procedures include:

- monitoring the funder's operations to identify and assess potential conflicting interests;
- disclosing conflicts of interest to funded parties and potential funded parties; and
- protecting their interests.

Similarly, the 2019 Abu Dhabi Litigation Funding Rules include provisions on conflicts of interest, stating:

> *the Litigation Funding Agreement must not contain any terms that: (a) could induce the Funded Party's lawyer or law firm to breach their professional duties which are owed to the Funded Party or to Abu Dhabi Global Market (ADGM) Courts including under the ADGM Courts Rules of Conduct; or (b) ... allow the Funder to influence the lawyer or law firm so that it takes control of the dispute or assumes conduct of it ...*

Many developments have taken place and many more will follow. What is certain is that third-party funding is here to stay.

> *Litigation Funding Agreements which include more than one Funded Party must include provisions for managing conflicts of interest between the Funder, the Funded Parties and the lawyers.*[88]

5. Conclusion

The treatment of third-party funding in different jurisdictions around the world has come a long way. Many jurisdictions now recognise the benefits that third-party funding can provide and its importance within the judicial system, including the international arbitration system. Many developments have taken place and many more will follow. What is certain is that third-party funding is here to stay. This is evident not only from the significant body of domestic legislation and international arbitration rules addressing third-party funding that has already emerged, but also from the increased demand for third-party funding in both litigation and arbitration. More importantly, there are now a number of national court decisions recognising that:

- third-party funding fees in international arbitration may be recovered as 'other costs'; and
- properly conducted, third-party funding is actually in the public interest of a society because it facilitates access to justice.

As Lord Neuberger, former president of the UK Supreme Court, has said, third-party funding is the "life-blood of the justice system".[89]

Notes

1 Some suggest that the practice of a third party not involved in a litigation providing financial assistance to a litigant originated in ancient Greek and Roman civil trials. See "The Ancient Origins of Third-Party Litigation Funding", *Delex,* 4 June 2021, https://delex.legal/the-ancient-origins-of-third-party-litigation-funding/#_ftn5.
2 *Ibid.*
3 See L Alakija, "Nigeria's New Arbitration Act: What You Need to Know", Kluwer Arbitration Blog, 25 June 2023, https://arbitrationblog.kluwerarbitration.com/2023/06/25/nigerias-new-arbitration-act-what-you-need-to-know/.
4 See Section 61 of the Nigerian Arbitration and Mediation Act 2023, www.lawyard.org/wp-content/uploads/2023/05/Arbitration-and-Mediation-Act.pdf.
5 *Ibid,* Section 63(2) www.lawyard.org/wp-content/uploads/2023/05/Arbitration-and-Mediation-Act.pdf.
6 *Persona Digital Telephony Limited v Minister for Public Enterprise* [2017] IESC 27.
7 *Ibid.* This was observed by Justice Clarke – see para 2.8, www.supremecourt.ie/Judgments.nsf/1b0757edc371032e802572ea0061450e/dcde288aae8fd4c4802581290038dbc0?OpenDocument.
8 For example, Justice McKechnie noted that it would be preferable to defer the making of an order on this matter until the state has been able to address "the deeply disturbing situation of the appellants being unable to prosecute this action solely because of the continuing existence of ancient principles of law, such as those of maintenance and champerty".
9 See, eg, H McEntee, "Third-Party Arbitration Funding to be Legalised in Ireland", *Irish Legal News,* 19 September 2022, www.irishlegal.com/articles/third-party-arbitration-funding-to-be-legalised-in-ireland.
10 Courts and Civil Law (Miscellaneous Provisions) Act 2023, www.irishstatutebook.ie/eli/2023/act/18/enacted/en/print.
11 *Ibid*, Section 5A(2).
12 *Ibid*, Section 5A(3).
13 See www.lawreform.ie/_fileupload/Executive%20Summaries/CP%2069%202023%20-%20Ex%20Summary%20Only.pdf.
14 See M Chan, M Secomb and P Tan, "Third-Party Funding: A New Chapter in Hong Kong & Singapore", *JD Supra*, 29 July 2016.

15 The Civil Law (Amendment) Act 2017 was passed by Parliament on 10 January 2017. See A Henderson and D Waldek, "Singapore Arbitration Update: Third-Party Funding and New SIAC Rules 2016", *Herbert Smith Freehills Arbitration Notes*, 1 July 2016, https://hsfnotes.com/arbitration/2016/07/01/singapore-arbitration-update-third-party-funding-and-new-siac-rules-2016/.
16 Regulation 4 of the Civil Law (Third-Party Funding) Regulations of 2017.
17 Section 2 of the Civil Law (Amendment) Act 2017 to amend the Civil Law Act (Chapter 43 of the 1999 Revised Edition) and to make a related amendment to the Legal Profession Act (Chapter 161 of the 2009 Revised Edition), passed 10 January 2017 and assented by the president on 3 February 2017.
18 It is currently unclear in Hong Kong whether the doctrines of maintenance and champerty apply to third-party funding for arbitrations taking place in Hong Kong: see the Court of Final Appeal judgment in *Unruh v Seeberger* (2007) 10 HKCFAR 31, at para 123, where the court expressly left open this question. While earlier in *Cannonway Consultants Limited v Kenworth Engineering Ltd*, [1995] 2 HKLR 475, Judge Kaplan had held that the law of champerty did not extend to arbitration, later in *Unruh v Seeberger*, (2007) 10 HKCFAR 31, at para 123, the court did not refer to this aspect of Kaplan's judgment. Accordingly, the permissibility of third-party funding with respect to arbitration in Hong Kong has been subject to uncertainty. See Law Reform Commission of Hong Kong, *Final Report on Third-party Funding for Arbitration*, October 2016, para 1.6, www.hkreform.gov.hk/en/publications/rtpf.htm.
19 See Draft Code of Practice for Third-Party Funding of Arbitration and Mediation, www.gov.hk/en/residents/government/publication/consultation/docs/2018/tpfcode.pdf.
20 *Ibid*, Article 2.5.
21 *Ibid,* Article 2.9.
22 See the High Level Committee Report, https://legalaffairs.gov.in/sites/default/files/Report-HLC.pdf, pp43–44.
23 *Tomorrow Sales Agency Private Limited v SBS Holdings, Inc*, 2023:DHC:3830-DB, http://164.100.69.66/jsearch/judgement.php?path=dhc/VIB/judgement/29-05-2023/&name=VIB29052023FAC592023_190809.pdf, pp29–30.
24 See Code of Conduct for Litigation Funders, January 2018, https://associationoflitigationfunders.com/wp-content/uploads/2018/03/Code-Of-Conduct-for-Litigation-Funders-at-Jan-2018-FINAL.pdf.
25 The enactment was effected under Sections 225(3)(a) and (d) of the Abu Dhabi Global Markets Courts, Civil Evidence, Judgments, Enforcement and Judicial Appointments Regulations 2015.
26 See Article 5 of the rules, www.adgm.com/documents/courts/legislation-and-procedures/legislation/rules/litigation-funding-rules-2019.pdf.
27 See *Campbells Cash and Carry Pty Ltd v Fostif Pty Ltd* [2006] HCA 41; 299 CLR 286, https://jade.io/article/1499.
28 See the government's press release of 22 May 2020, "Litigation Funders to be Regulated under the Corporations Act", https://ministers.treasury.gov.au/ministers/josh-frydenberg-2018/media-releases/litigation-funders-be-regulated-under-corporations.
29 See the Explanatory Statement issued by the Treasurer, www5.austlii.edu.au/au/legis/cth/num_reg_es/cafr2020202000942551.html.
30 See European Parliament resolution of 13 September 2022 with recommendations to the Commission on responsible private funding of litigation (2020/2130INL), para 14, www.europarl.europa.eu/doceo/document/TA-9-2022-0308_EN.html#title1.
31 See www.europarl.europa.eu/doceo/document/TA-9-2022-0308_EN.html#title1.
32 See ILFA, *Resourcing the Rule of Law in Europe*, June 2023, https://uploads-ssl.webflow.com/5ef44d9ad0e366e4767c9f0c/6498d39ac7b645dcdc5b9a4d_Resourcing%20the%20Rule%20of%20Law%20in%20Europe_Full%20report.pdf.
33 *Ibid*, p4.
34 D Haughan and S Friel, "Litigation Funding", *Lexology*, 21 November 2023, www.lexology.com/library/detail.aspx?g=b21a950a-0e92-4998-93e7-4ce6f0eda8ce.
35 This confusion is apparent even at a terminological level. As one commentator describes: "The nomenclature to describe this kind of third-party capital investment in arbitration or litigation claims is all over the map and woefully undescriptive. It has been referred to as 'third-party funding', 'third-party litigation funding or financing', or most commonly 'alternative litigation funding or financing'". M Destefano, "Non-Lawyers Influencing Lawyers: Too Many Cooks in the Kitchen or Stone Soup", 80 *Fordham Law Review* (2012) p2791 at p2794.
36 For example, Sections 98K to 98N of the Hong Kong Arbitration and Mediation Legislation (Third-Party Funding) (Amendment Ordinance) expressly permit third-party funding for arbitration, mediation and related litigation under the Arbitration Ordinance (Cap 609). Sections 98K and 98L provide that the common law offences of maintenance (including champerty) and barratry and the tort of maintenance (including champerty) do not apply to third-party funding of arbitration. However, Section 98O provides that these amendments to Hong Kong law do not apply to the provision of funding to a party by a lawyer acting for any parties in relation to such arbitration, mediation and related litigation proceedings. This exclusion suggests that, in the absence of such an exclusion, the Hong Kong definition of 'third-party funding' could include lawyer funding through contingency fees (although Section 64 of the Legal Practitioners Ordinance (Cap 159) prohibits solicitors from purchasing an interest in a client's contentious proceedings or agreeing to charge success fees for contentious work). See also Section 107(3A) read with Section 107(3B) of the Legal

Profession Act, and Rule 49B of the Legal Profession (Professional Conduct) Rules 2015 (Singapore).
37 See AJ Sebok, "The Inauthentic Claim", 64 *Vanderbilt Law Review* (2011) p61, at pp63–67. See C Veljanovski, "Third-Party Litigation Funding in Europe", 8 *Journal of Law, Economics and Policy* (2011) p405 at p430 ("[Third-party litigation funding investors] rely on Special Purpose Vehicles, which ... are legal entities created for ... the acquisition, financing, or both, of a project or the setup of an investment. They are usually used because they are free from pre-existing obligations and debts and are separate from the parties that set them up for tax and insolvency purposes").
38 For example, just as excessive repeat appointment of an individual arbitrator by a party or law firm can be a basis for challenging that arbitrator, under the IBA Guidelines on Conflicts of Interest in International Arbitration, repeat appointment of an arbitrator by the same third-party funder can raise similar challenges. See IBA Guidelines 3.1.3. If funding is done through an SPV created for the particular case, it may mask the repeated appointment by a particular third-party funder that owns the SPV.
39 See M Kantor, "Third-Party Funding in International Arbitration: An Essay About New Developments", 24 *ICSID Review* (2009) p65 at p74; JA Trusz, "Full Disclosure? Conflicts of Interest Arising from Third-Party Funding in International Commercial Arbitration", 101 *The Georgetown Law Journal* (2013) p1649 at p1654.
40 See press release by Uruguay's Counsel, Foley Hoag LLP, "Government of Uruguay Taps Foley Hoag for Representation in International Arbitration Brought by Philip Morris to Overturn Country's Tobacco Regulations", October 2010, www.prnewswire.com/news-releases/government-of-uruguay-taps-foley-hoag-for-representation-in-international-arbitration-brought-by-philip-morris-to-overturn-countrys-tobacco-regulations-104599339.html.
41 See FC Diaz, "RSM Production Corp. Files Second Arbitration against Grenada, Sues Freshfields", *Investment Treaty News*, 8 April 2010, www.iisd.org/itn/2010/04/08/rsm-production-corp-files-second-arbitration-against-grenada-sues-freshfields/.
42 Article 27(1) of the CIETAC Rules.
43 See 2021 International Chamber of Commerce (ICC) Rules, para 21, https://iccwbo.org/content/uploads/sites/3/2020/12/icc-note-to-parties-and-arbitral-tribunals-on-the-conduct-of-arbitration-english-2021.pdf.
44 See Article 14(1) of the ICSID Arbitration Rules.
45 See www.foris.com/en/about-us/.
46 See https://omnibridgeway.com/about/overview#History.
47 J Kalajdzic, P Cashman and A Longmoore, "Justice for Profit: A Comparative Analysis of Australian Canadian and U.S. Third Party Litigation Funding", 61 *American Journal of Comparative Law* 93, 95 (2013); See also JJ Stroble and L Welikson, "Third-Party Litigation Funding: A Review of Recent Industry Developments", *Defense Counsel Journal*, January 2020, www.iadclaw.org/assets/1/17/Third-Party_Litigation_Funding_-_A_Review_of_Recent_Industry_Developments2.pdf.
48 See https://sentryfunding.co.uk/insights/the-history-of-litigation-funding/.
49 See www.legislation.gov.uk/ukpga/1990/41/contents.
50 See www.legislation.gov.uk/ukpga/1999/22/contents.
51 Since then, there have been two further developments: one in 2005 (Conditional Fee Agreements (Revocation) Regulations 2005, SI 2005/2305) and one in 2012 following the introduction of the Jackson Reform (Legal Aid, Sentencing and Punishment of Offenders Act 2012, Section 44).
52 See, eg, *R (on the application of Factortame) v Secretary of State for Transport, Environment and the Regions (No 2)* [2002] EWCA Civ 932 and *Arkin v Borchard Lines* [2005] EWCA Civ 655.
53 *R (on the application of PACCAR Inc) v Competition Appeal Tribunal* [2023] UKSC 28 on appeal from: [2021] EWCA Civ 299, www.supremecourt.uk/cases/docs/uksc-2021-0078-judgment.pdf.
54 This means satisfying the requirements set out in the Damages-Based Agreements Regulations 2013.
55 *R (on the application of PACCAR Inc) v Competition Appeal Tribunal* [2023] UKSC 28, para 1.3
56 C Bogart, "Third-Party Funding in International Arbitration", *International Chamber of Commerce Institute of World Business Law Dossier X*, 50, 55.
57 Nearly $10 billion in combined assets under management have been dedicated to US legal finance and, of that, $2.3 billion was committed to commercial litigation finance transactions with a nexus to the United States in 2019 alone. See *Business Wire*, "$2.3 Billion of Capital Deployed Over 12 Month Period Across U.S. Commercial Litigation Finance Industry According to First of Its Kind Study", 19 November 2019, www.businesswire.com/news/home/20191119005098/en/2.3-Billion-of-Capital-Deployed-Over-12-Month-Period-Across-U.S.-Commercial-Litigation-Finance-Industry-According-to-First-of-Its-Kind-Study; see also Woodsford, "Funding for International Arbitration", https://woodsford.com/wp-content/uploads/2022/09/Funding-for-International-Arbitration.pdf.
58 See FTI Consulting, "The Decade of Disputes and the Impact of Litigation Funding", https://fticommunications.com/wp-content/uploads/2021/07/FTI-Consulting-The-Decade-of-Disputes-The-Impact-of-Litigation-Funding.pdf; see also G Stevenson and P Taylor, "What's Behind the Rapid Growth of Third-Party Litigation Funding", AlixPartners, 6 July 2021, https://insights.alixpartners.com/post/102h2d2/whats-behind-the-rapid-growth-of-third-party-litigation-funding.
59 See press release, "Litigation Funders Backing Class Action Lawsuits as They Put £2.2bn 'War Chests' to Work", RPC, 20 June 2022, www.rpc.co.uk/press-and-media/litigation-funders-backing-class-action-lawsuits-as-they-put-22bn-war-chests-to-work/.
60 See R Wheal and O Dean, "The End of the Regulatory Vacuum in Europe and a New Era for

International Arbitration in Ireland? Developments in Third-Party Funding Regulation", White & Case, 27 October 2022, www.whitecase.com/insight-alert/end-regulatory-vacuum-europe-and-new-era-international-arbitration-ireland.
61 See Special Report, "The Rise of Third-Party Funding in International Arbitration", *Financier Worldwide*, October 2016, www.financierworldwide.com/the-rise-of-third-party-funding-in-international-arbitration#.Y2PJsezP2WA.
62 See Queen Mary University of London and PwC Study 2013, "Corporate Choices in International Arbitration: Industry Perspectives" (https://arbitration.qmul.ac.uk/research/2013/); and Queen Mary and White & Case Studies 2015, "Improvements and Innovations in International Arbitration" (https://arbitration.qmul.ac.uk/research/2015/) and 2018, "International Arbitration Survey: The Evolution of International Arbitration" (https://arbitration.qmul.ac.uk/research/2018/); see also G Stevenson and P Taylor, "What's Behind the Rapid Growth of Third-Party Litigation Funding?" AlixPartners, 6 July 2021, https://insights.alixpartners.com/post/102h2d2/whats-behind-the-rapid-growth-of-third-party-litigation-funding.
63 Sixty-one per cent of the 101 surveyed in-house counsel had agreed on capped hourly fees with outside counsel in arbitration cases; 27% had used discounted hourly rates plus a success fee calculated as a percentage of the damages awarded or recovered; 22% had used discounted hourly rates plus a success fee calculated as a percentage of outside counsel's hourly fee; and 10% had used pure contingency fees. Twenty per cent had resorted to BTE insurance. Only 6% had contracted with litigation funders. See pp5, 19–20, https://arbitration.qmul.ac.uk/research/2013/.
64 See Queen Mary University of London and White & Case Survey 2015, "Improvements and Innovations in International Arbitration", https://arbitration.qmul.ac.uk/media/arbitration/docs/2015_International_Arbitration_Survey.pdf, pp45–46.
65 *Ibid*, p45. Only 15% of respondents had encountered such insurance products in practice: 3% had used them; and 12% had seen them used.
66 *Ibid*, p46.
67 According to the Queen Mary University of London and White & Case Survey 2018, only 3% of the respondents were not aware of it; 56% were aware of it but had not seen it used in practice; 26% had seen it used in practice; and 16% had used it in practice, https://arbitration.qmul.ac.uk/media/arbitration/docs/2018-International-Arbitration-Survey—-The-Evolution-of-International-Arbitration-(2).PDF, p24.
68 *Ibid*, pp24–25.
69 *Ibid*, p25.
70 *Ibid*, p24.
71 See Queen Mary University of London and White & Case Survey 2021, "International Arbitration Survey: Adapting Arbitration in a Changing World", https://arbitration.qmul.ac.uk/media/arbitration/docs/LON0320037-QMUL-International-Arbitration-Survey-2021_19_WEB.pdf, p8.
72 Article 24(l) of the 2017 SIAC Investment Arbitration Rules.
73 Article 27(2) of the CIETAC Rules.
74 See, eg, Articles 4.3(i), 5(1)(g), 27(6)(i), 27(7)(f) and Article 44; this obligation applies throughout the whole arbitration irrespective of when such an arrangement was made.
75 Article 13(a) provides that parties "shall disclose the existence of any third-party funding and the identity of third party funder in its statement of claim or its answer to the statement of claim, or immediately upon concluding a third-party funding agreement".
76 Under Article 11(7) of the ICC Rules, parties are required to "promptly inform" the tribunal, the secretariat and the other party of the "existence and identity of any non-party which has entered into an arrangement for the funding of claims or defences and under which it has an economic interest in the outcome of the arbitration". This is necessary in order to "assist" the arbitrators in complying with their duties.
77 Article 27 requires the disclosure of the third-party agreement, if one is entered into, as well as the identity of the funder.
78 Article 14(1) of the 2022 ICSID Arbitration Rules.
79 See also a study by AlixPartners and *The Lawyer*, "The Future of Third Party Litigation Funding" 2021, www.alixpartners.com/media/17916/litigation-funding-survey-2021-tl.pdf; See also EY's Forensic & Integrity Services Survey, "How Covid Has Impacted the UK's Claims and Disputes Landscape", 19 April 2021, www.ey.com/en_uk/assurance/how-covid-19-impacts-the-claims-and-disputes-landscape.
80 According to EY's Forensic & Integrity Services Survey, "How Covid Has Impacted the UK's Claims and Disputes Landscape", both corporates (70%) and lawyers (92%) indicated that the most influential factor, when deciding whether to pursue a claim over the next 12 months, would be the ongoing need to navigate the business impact of COVID-19 as a priority. The second most influential factor (as reported by 62% of corporates) was the need to protect shareholder value, www.ey.com/en_uk/assurance/how-covid-19-impacts-the-claims-and-disputes-landscape.
81 See EY Survey, "How the Pandemic is Changing Attitudes Towards Third-Party Funding", 12 May 2021, www.ey.com/en_uk/assurance/how-the-pandemic-is-changing-attitudes-towards-third-party-funding.
82 *Ibid*.
83 See N Marigo, "Third-Party Funding: Easing into the Mainstream", Freshfields 2022, www.freshfields.com/490835/globalassets/our-thinking/campaigns/arbitration-top-trends-2022/international_arbitration_top_trends_2022.pdf.

84 *Ibid*; see also AlixPartners and *The Lawyer*, "The Future of Third Party Litigation Funding" 2021, www.alixpartners.com/media/17916/litigation-funding-survey-2021-tl.pdf.
85 See FTI Consulting, "Third-Party Funding: A Source of Capital for Any Company With a Good Legal Claim", 28 April 2022, www.fticonsulting.com/emea/insights/articles/third-party-funding-source-capital-any-company-with-good-legal-claim.
86 See Standard 7(a) of the IBA Guidelines on Conflicts of Interest in International Arbitration, www.ibanet.org/MediaHandler?id=e2fe5e72-eb14-4bba-b10d-d33dafee8918.
87 See Draft Code of Practice for Third-Party Funding of Arbitration and Mediation, www.gov.hk/en/residents/government/publication/consultation/docs/2018/tpfcode.pdf.
88 See Article 9 of the 2019 Abu Dhabi Litigation Funding Rules, www.adgm.com/documents/courts/legislation-and-procedures/legislation/rules/litigation-funding-rules-2019.pdf.
89 See Neuberger, "From Barretry, Maintenance and Champerty to Litigation Funding", Harbour Litigation Funding First Annual Lecture, 8 May 2013, www.supremecourt.uk/docs/speech-130508.pdf.

II. Types of litigation funding options available

Matthew Amey
TheJudge

1. Introduction

Litigation funding is gaining more recognition as a means of claim holders exploiting the contingent value of a single case or portfolio of claims in order to finance the costs of proceedings. However, there are several other types of transactions where the contingent value of a legal dispute can be used as an asset which allows a claim holder to access funds prior to a success crystallising in a recovery of value for the claim holder.

This chapter endorses a wide definition of the term 'litigation funding'. Arrangements whereby professional financiers advance cash to pay for legal costs in return for a success fee paid back to them from the contingent proceeds which flow from a successful outcome in the funded case are commonly understood. However, this is just one of a range of transactions designed to support legal proceedings by mitigating the costs and risks for claim holders. Different instruments include insurance and alternative billing arrangements offered by lawyers, neither of which typically involves the advancement of cash. While not strictly 'funding legal costs' under a narrow definition, these are certainly no less valuable or worthy of discussion. One of the most ubiquitous – insurance – is explored below.

2. Insurance

Companies, institutions and individuals offering funding for litigation and arbitration are in the business of trading risk. The word 'funding' emphasises the provision of cash flow, but the dominant purpose of most transactions is to reduce or remove risk of the claim holder. A traditional[1] litigation funding arrangement has a dual role: both to fund the necessary legal costs and to remove the risk of those costs from the claim holder.

Many claimants are completely reliant on a funder's agreement to meet its legal costs up to settlement or trial. Others approach funders to weigh up the option of using their own resources versus sharing the risk with a funder in return for relinquishing a share of the contingent proceeds. Claimants that are risk averse but have the resources to pay their costs can consider options that concentrate on risk sharing above the advancement of cash. When it comes to sharing risk, there is no better marketplace than the insurance industry, because of its unique combination of appetite for risk and low cost of capital. Generally, insurers can take risks in return for premiums that specialist funders cannot because of their comparative size, diversification of exposures, transaction volume, investment strategies and access to reinsurance.

Companies, institutions and individuals offering funding for litigation and arbitration are in the business of trading risk.

There are several different forms of litigation insurance, so perhaps it is best to start with a list of products accompanied by a short description.

2.1 Before-the-event insurance

Before-the-event (BTE) insurance is a product that covers the legal costs risk of a dispute that might arise in the future. Such products can:

- provide an indemnity for costs in the event that a case fails; or
- in some instances, pay for costs incurred before the final conclusion (a rare example of insurers advancing cash).

2.2 After-the-event insurance

After-the-event (ATE) insurance is a product that covers the legal costs risk of a dispute that has already arisen (hence the differentiation between BTE and ATE).[2] The policies provide cover for two types of legal costs, as follows.

(a) Adverse costs/fee shifting insurance

This covers the risk of having to pay the opponent's legal costs in the event of losing the case (by order of the court or tribunal) or discontinuing the case with costs payable to the opponent by agreement. These policies will often cover the costs consequences of failing to beat a formal offer of settlement.

ATE insurance is frequently used as a solution to satisfy (or avoid) an order for security to protect a defendant/respondent's costs. A 'bare ATE' policy may be accepted as security, but generally it is anticipated that for an ATE insurance policy to constitute adequate security, the insurer must agree to modify the policy to provide a high level of comfort that the opponent will be paid by the insurer directly notwithstanding any breach of the terms and conditions by the policyholder (against which the insurer may still have recourse).

Such modifications are called 'anti-avoidance endorsements'. Alternatively, the insurer may enter into a direct contractual agreement with the opponent through a deed of indemnity that runs in parallel with the policy.

(b) Own costs insurance

This provides an indemnity for own costs incurred to bring a claim. This will often be limited to disbursements such as expert costs or court/tribunal fees, but can include the lawyer's basic fees and barrister's fees.

Own costs products may be purchased by the claim holder pursuant to a negotiated arrangement with the instructed lawyer, who agrees to defer their charges until the proceedings conclude. This means that the lawyer's entitlements to fees or expenses come from the proceeds upon success or, in the alternative, from a claim on the insurance policy made by their client.

Effectively, this form of insurance enables the client to encourage the law firm to help fund the case.

2.3 Contingency fee insurance

In permissible jurisdictions, and where economically viable, a law firm may assume its client's legal costs risk under a contingency fee arrangement (known as a 'damages-based agreement' in the UK) or a conditional fee arrangement (CFA). Contingency fee insurance is, unlike all the other forms of legal expenses insurance products, available to a law firm acting on such a contingency. This form of insurance effectively underpins an arrangement for the law firm to fund (or partially fund) the case by covering:

- a percentage of the law firm's base fees notionally incurred on an hourly rate basis under the terms of its agreement with the client; and
- up to 100% of any 'hard costs' that the firm has agreed to fund.

The law firm can make a claim on the policy in the event that:

- the client's case loses; or
- the fees paid to the firm by the client under the CFA are less than the sums insured.

2.4 Litigation containment insurance/litigation buy-out insurance

In contrast to other funding products, litigation containment insurance is solely directed to parties defending disputes rather than bringing claims. The product is a species of the wider warranty and indemnity industry and allows a party at risk of a potentially very large award against it in the future to remove the risk of a catastrophic outcome. It must persuade an insurer that:

- the claim against it will never arise or never succeed; or
- if the claim does succeed, the award will be small.

There is often external pressure to purchase a policy such as this – for example, pressure from a buyer for a vendor to cap a remote risk in order for an acquisition of the vendor to proceed.

Another point of differentiation is that this type of insurance is not limited to the defendant's legal costs. The bulk, if not all, of the risk insured is some part of the claim value awarded against the policyholder.

2.5 Arbitration default insurance

An insurer will assume the risk, up to a limit, of a sovereign state respondent to an international arbitration failing to pay an award against it within a specified timeframe. The insurance is usually purchased well before the outcome of the arbitration is known and if there is no award, the insurer is off-risk. In that way, unlike all other forms of litigation funding, the insurer's interest might be seen to be at odds with that of the claim holder, as the former does not necessarily want the insured to obtain an award.

Again, this policy covers the award itself and is not limited to a policy for legal costs.

2.6 Cross-undertaking in damages insurance

Cross-undertakings are necessary to obtain an interim remedy, such as a freezing injunction, that could itself cause the opponent a loss. Insurance policies are available to protect an applicant from the consequences of having to pay an opponent under such an undertaking.

An insurer will assume the risk, up to a limit, of a sovereign state respondent to an international arbitration failing to pay an award against it within a specified timeframe.

For international arbitrations, ATE insurance and contingency fee insurance are by far the most relevant. This is both because they directly address major funding issues for claim holders and because the majority of the premium is usually deferred and contingent, which is often critical to completing the funding package necessary to allow international arbitrations to proceed.

2.7 Contingent premiums

Most insurance policies require the payment of a premium upfront on inception of the policy. In contrast, ATE insurance and contingency fee insurance usually involve a premium that is payable only from the recovered proceeds. By definition, the premium is therefore contingent upon success and recovery. This makes ATE insurance and contingency fee insurance a match for litigation funding insofar as risk taking is concerned, albeit that they do not pay cash during the life of a case – the exception being claims for interim adverse costs awards made on ATE insurance policies.

Unlike litigation funding, some ATE policies require a premium payable upfront on inception (often known as 'deposit premium'), with the balance payable on a contingent basis. Moreover, the contingent premium payable is usually staged such that the amount increases depending on the stage the legal process reaches. This keeps the premium proportionate to the amount of the insurer's actual exposure to the real-time legal budget but also aids settlement.

3. Monetisation

Contingent litigation proceeds have balance-sheet value before the outcome of the litigation. If that value is realised in the form of a settlement or an award, finance providers contract for recourse to some of those proceeds. Thus, litigation funding in its widest sense can be used for various finance needs beyond the provision of legal costs of a dispute.

Monetisation arrangements emanate from funders advancing cash against judgment debts. A funder will pay so many 'cents in the dollar' and commit to an enforcement budget to see the court judgment or tribunal award enforced. Some funders have reached further back into the legal process to monetise cases before judgment.

Such transactions can be a passive monetisation agreement between the claim holder and an external funder, where such an arrangement is legally permissible – for instance, an agreement for the funder to buy a share of the economic rights where the claim remains with the original claimant. Alternatively, it might entail a more active role for the funder, which could take an assignment of the claim itself or even buy shares in the entity that owns the claim, such that the funder exerts greater control.

Funders specialising in areas of practice such as insolvency and patent litigation are proficient at finding ways to release future claim value to their counterparties through monetisation.

Funders specialising in areas of practice such as insolvency and patent litigation are proficient at finding ways to release future claim value to their counterparties through monetisation. For insolvency practitioners, it can mean a quick distribution for creditors; and for patent owners, it can be a shortcut to real cash based on anticipated future revenue from licensing revenues if the patent is enforceable.

4. Broker role

Litigation insurance and litigation funding comprise a specialist market in which the participants, the products, the regulations and perspectives of best practice are constantly shifting. This may be attributable to how young the marketplace is compared to more traditional forms of insurance and finance. This means that individuals and organisations that have detailed, up-to-date information on the market can provide a valuable service to parties that need access to the market. Brokers are adept at finding niche areas and helping their clients to exploit the potential that such niche markets have to offer.

Brokers primarily identify and introduce interested parties with which their clients can transact. Some provide advice and assistance on how to present information about the case in order to secure an offer(s).

The intermediation and provision of insurance are regulated activities in jurisdictions around the globe. In contrast, the arrangement and delivery of litigation funding are almost entirely unregulated.[3] This impacts the role played by intermediaries, the demand for such services and the value-add that a broker can have when searching for and advising on suitable arrangements.

4.1 Insurance broking

The relationship between an insurance broker and its client is heavily regulated and the client has recourse to supervisory and complaint bodies, and potentially compensation schemes, for certain defaults by the broker. Requirements for the broker's conduct, process and capital adequacy vary; but in general, a broker is expected to gather information about the client's requirements and seek to match those needs to a suitable product. Brokers are likely to be obliged to explain:

- why they are recommending a particular product; and
- whether they have sourced the insurance offer from:
    - a single source;
    - a finite selection (or panel);
    - the whole market; or
    - a sample of insurers that represent the range of relevant providers from the market (a 'fair analysis' of the market).

In the world of litigation finance, the dividing line between brokers and funders is not always clear. Some intermediaries act as advisers to the party seeking funding, while others are 'introducers' acting on behalf of funders.

Lawyers will often outsource the role of searching for insurance to limit their professional exposure, but also because litigation insurance is a highly specialised product, often heavily tailored to the specific circumstances of the dispute. An insurance broker is usually paid a commission deducted from the insurance premium once it is payable to the insurer. As the vast majority of written premium is contingent upon success in the cases, the commission revenue is also contingent.

4.2 Litigation funding broking

In the world of litigation finance, the dividing line between brokers and funders is not always clear. Some intermediaries act as advisers to the party seeking funding, while others are 'introducers' acting on behalf of funders. Some organisations look and act like funders when in fact they raise money on each case from external investors on an *ad hoc* basis. This does not make them broker agents, but they are middlemen. If the outcome is a competitive funding solution, the role of the actors may not interest the litigants in need of funds, but lawyers should always ascertain whether they are dealing with an agent or a counterparty. If the former, lawyers should clarify to whom that entity owes its duties; if the latter, lawyers should investigate whether that entity has the money within its direct control.

The payment terms of litigation funding brokers vary significantly. Some are paid on success in line with the funder's success fee (eg, a percentage of the success return component); others are paid on closing of the transaction. Moreover, some intermediary fees paid on closing form part of the funder's commitment such that the funded party is borrowing the commission to pay the intermediary, so a success return will be added to the commission on success – this may double or triple the ultimate cost of the introduction service in the long run.

Notes

1 The use of the word 'traditional' is potentially misleading in an industry where what is considered the norm changes so quickly due to the influences of courts, governing bodies and the wider economy.

2 'ATE' is a misnomer. The event being insured is the outcome of the dispute whereas BTE covers the event of a dispute arising at all.

3 At least that is the case at the time of writing. While the UK market is self-regulating via the optional Association of Litigation Funders, in other jurisdictions there is pressure for external regulation. For example, the European Parliament voted in September 2022 in support of the recommendations of a report by German Member of the European Parliament Axel Voss to produce 'common minimum standards' across member states for Europe's commercial litigation funders.

III. Pre-funding considerations

Harshiv Thakerar
Asertis

This chapter examines the considerations for funders before they commit to an investment decision and how the funding agreement is used to best protect that decision.

Section 1 provides insight into the mechanics and emotion (yes, emotion plays a real part) behind any funding decision. Section 2 explains what funders are trying to protect against in any funding agreement, and the considerations made by each party to reach a deal and properly manage the relationship going forward.

1. Analysis of risk

Fundamentally, each investment in a claim is some form of debt and equity transaction. The funder is an investor, just like any other, investing in the execution of a theory of harm with a group of individuals (often wrapped as a corporate). The risk is full loss of capital; the return is (at least for the most part) first priority (akin to debt) and usually high or enhanced to reflect the risk (closer to equity). It is important to set out early that we do not discuss non-commercial or non-fundable claims here.

1.1 Risks and rewards for claim participants

The participants involved in any claim (excluding the funder) include the claimant's law firm, counsel (if external to the law firm), after-the-event insurer and broker. I refer to these participants as the 'claim constituents'. Of course, there are other players in the journey of a claim – such as experts and witnesses – who do not participate in the risk/reward analysis and must remain non-incentivised to do so. I must also be clear here that I am referring specifically to jurisdictions in which law firms and counsel are allowed to take risk on claims, such as England.

The claim is the 'theory', and the claim constituents will want to properly formulate, articulate and ultimately successfully exit the transaction based on the theory. For the funder in this scenario to be able to commit to the investment, it needs to assess risk against reward:

- Risk: The full loss of capital and potentially more if there is an adverse costs order against the funder.
- Reward: Either a percentage of the recoveries or a multiple on the investment.

The participants in the risk/reward consideration in a funded claim are not just the funder. They must include all the claim constituents; otherwise, there could be a fundamental misalignment which could lead to missteps at any point in the journey – most likely closer to exit. There is, of course, variance in the risks (and hence degrees of variance between how the risk is assessed) between the claim constituents.

Law firms and counsel in England primarily participate by:

- deferring a portion of their fees in exchange for a fee uplift on successful resolution (a conditional fee agreement (CFA)); or
- taking a percentage of the overall award (a damages-based agreement (DBA)).

However, the law firm and counsel will almost always ask to be paid 'on the run' by the funder during the lifetime of the litigation and will carry a limited risk on a contingent basis depending on recoveries in the litigation.

An insurer will be paid a premium for taking the risk up to a limit of indemnity and will participate in the claim revenue (depending on the terms of the insurance) with a deferred and contingent further premium. The contingent element will be dependent on recovery of any damages and costs awarded in the claim. But the major risk that insurers are protecting against is the pay-out of an adverse costs award in the event of loss. Therefore, for an insurer, if the claim loses (or wins but cannot be enforced) and it does not have to pay out any of the risk on cover, that can be considered a 'win'.

1.2 Considerations for funders

Funders generally provide all of the capital for a claim, from inception of the funding agreement to conclusion of the trial or beyond. Depending on the structure of the funder, its income can often solely derive from the success of a claim. This may seem like an obvious statement, but it is not always the case. I will not go into detail here about the different ways in which funders are structured; suffice to say that some funders 'manage' a fund or funds on behalf of investors and take a management fee for doing so (which can be a profitable enterprise in itself). However, we will assume for the purpose of this chapter that all funders depend on the success of their investments to make an income.

On-balance-sheet funders, which do not manage funds for external parties, will often owe an accrued interest payment to their investors (usually calculated on an internal rate-of-return basis so that it compounds annually) and will have to cover any losses, other operational and due diligence expenses and accruing interest from wins. A quick reminder: funders operate on a non-recourse basis, so if the claim loses, they have no recompense for the cash they have spent.

Funders generally provide all of the capital for a claim, from inception of the funding agreement to conclusion of the trial or beyond.

Therefore, the reward (determined by pricing) of any one claim must reflect this myriad of risks and costs. It really is a zero-sum game. So, for a funder to be comfortable investing in a claim, it must be satisfied on a number of factors:

- Belief in the merits (liability, causation and quantum): Merit is the issue most often discussed in any funding arrangement, but in reality it is only one factor. Even the best claims on merits have inherent litigation (uncertainty of trial due to witness evidence, legal team performance, judgment error, adverse costs risk) and recovery risks. Some funders pore over every detail in a claim to glean their own views on the merits; some take a broad-brush approach and fund as many claims as they can; and some fund only certain types of claims and review merits in less detail than others. Broadly, however, funders will take advice on the merits of a claim and decide whether it meets their own merits threshold.
- Ability to enforce the claim (quantum plays a factor here, but the likelihood of the defendant paying by way of enforcement action or settlement is key): Enforcement is as important a factor as any. As a general rule, a funder cannot recover its funding costs from the other side, except through the ultimate recovered damages and costs. Exceptions include arbitration claims in which certain institutional rules may empower arbitrators to order a party to pay the funding costs of the winning claimant. A final consideration that is sometimes overlooked by those seeking funding is not just the ability to enforce, but also how much of this can be enforced. What is the defendant's 'financial pain' threshold, which will force it to go to trial rather than being able to settle, or which may make it insolvent?
- Economic metrics (for successful resolution): Linked to the enforcement consideration is the overall economics of the claim. Will the realistic claim value tolerate the investment and final cost of funding? As mentioned above, there are other risk/reward participants to be considered. Once all of these have been accounted for and realistic settlement values ascribed, how much will be left for the claimant(s)? Can they justify taking the funding or is the juice not worth the squeeze? Duration is key here for any funder. As mentioned above, funders are often paying compound interest on the money that they borrow. A claim that is likely to go on for five years will involve very different economic considerations from one that might only last for two.
- Settlement (push and pull factors on whether a claim might settle out of court): Funders should generally ensure that pricing means that the claimant will receive at least 50% of any

As a general rule, a funder cannot recover its funding costs from the other side, except through the ultimate recovered damages and costs.

damages in most resolution scenarios. There are varying statistics on settlement, but it is generally agreed that most commercial claims settle. Most claimants and defendants will agree that going to trial is risky and costly, which means that sensible heads often prevail. A funder will need to be comfortable that its own input will not adversely affect any settlement dynamic. Funders must also consider whether the claimant simply wants to have its day in court and is not minded to resolve the claim on a commercial basis.

- Risk alignment (between all parties): As alluded to above, there are many parties involved in this dynamic, which all need to be pulling in the same direction. Some funders don't care so much about this and will only seek to work on cases that they think are suitable due to the other factors discussed here. Others will require law firms or counsel to take material risk by deferring some of their fees in exchange for an uplift on those fees.
- Reputation (ethical considerations): Most funders are not in this industry to fund the odd claim and bank on a couple of cases paying out. They are in the industry for a more determined purpose and will therefore want to fund claims that they have reasonable belief in and that pass the 'good actor' test. They try not to fund claims where the claimant may not have the moral high ground.
- Portfolio management (the funder's current portfolio

composition and risk appetite): This is an important factor that many law firms and claimants may not fully appreciate. As with any market, there is limited capacity for certain allocations of funds. Even if a law firm comes forward with an ostensibly fantastic claim that is ready for funding, some funders simply may not have the immediate capacity to take it on. For example, they may have funded too many claims in that particular competition or arbitration space, or against a particular type of defendant, and simply cannot or do not wish to take any more risk in that area.

2. The funding agreement

In this section, I focus on funding agreements under English law. I am obliged to mention the recent Supreme Court decision in the *PACCAR* case.[1] It does have an impact on litigation funding, but it is by no means as 'catastrophic' or 'seismic' as suggested by some. At the time of writing, the implication is that one type of pricing method (percentage of damages) may not be deemed appropriate for calculating a funder's success fee. Funders retain other methods of pricing, such as multipliers on funds deployed or committed to a claim, internal rate of return or other interest rate calculations. The real difficulty here is for the claimant – funders have reacted to the case and will continue to do so, just as any other lender would have. It limits the pricing options available to claimants and may even push up overall pricing.

I discuss below some key common practices (outside of pricing) in the funding agreement. These are by no means exhaustive and indeed some funders may entertain entirely different views from mine.

Key considerations in funding agreements include the following:

- Gateways: These are crucial to the continued success of a claim. Essentially, they are individual hurdles (or gates) that must be passed to allow funding to continue. They relate to material risks in the claim and are a limited tool to allow funders to control the funding provided for the continuance of a claim. Some funders opt not to use gateways at all and instead choose an overarching material adverse change (MAC) clause. Other funders have detailed gateways that permit the release of certain amounts of funding only until a gateway is cleared. Some have a combination of both – there may be certain 'ongoing' gateways that will be akin to a MAC clause and there may be others that relate to specific instances. Specific instances can include:
  - milestones such as bookbuild (in a group action);
  - the results of a particular opinion or expert's report; or
  - even the continued participation of key witnesses or professionals.

- Representations and warranties: When making funding decisions, a funder can only rely on the theory and evidence provided by the claimant and lawyers. The funder will be investing significant sums of capital into a claim and must be comfortable that the claimant and lawyers have represented the claim to the fullest extent and that nothing has been hidden. More than one funder has had to rely on such representations and warranties in the face of evidence uncovered after investment. Funders will robustly and correctly defend their position if they have been wronged.
- Settlements and reasonable offers: As alluded to throughout, it is important that the claim constituents are as aligned as can be. While English law prevents control exerted by a funder, it is common practice for a funder to protect itself by inserting mechanisms by which reasonable offers in the advice of their law firm and counsel should be treated. If a claimant refuses to accept what might be deemed a reasonable offer, the first port of call will be a sensible discussion between all parties. If all parties still are not aligned, funders may ask for an independent review of the offer by a different counsel agreed between the parties.
- Budgeting and reporting: These two very important points

When making funding decisions, a funder can only rely on the theory and evidence provided by the claimant and lawyers.

have not been touched on so far. A funder should be as comfortable as possible with how much it is committing to a claim. It is incumbent on the law firm to provide a budget and manage it properly, and for the funder to monitor this. There may well be reasons for budget variations and proper reporting should avoid any strain on a relationship. In order to monitor budgetary risk together with the overall progress of the case, the funder will often have reporting requirements for the clients to manage the claim.

3. Conclusion

Analysis of risk/reward and alignment is absolutely essential for any funder and the funding agreement should reflect agreed views on risk mitigation. Funders can analyse risk well if they have all possible information available to them at the outset of the investment consideration and can take steps to mitigate via the funding agreement. Ongoing reporting and proper communication should obviate most difficult scenarios and lead to a successful relationship.

Notes

1 *R (on the application of PACCAR Inc) v Competition Appeal Tribunal* [2023] UKSC 28.

IV. Regulation of the funding market

Matthew Lo
Tom Steindler
Exton Advisors

1. Introduction

The global market for third-party funding (or 'litigation funding') has been on a journey from obscurity (or, in fact, in the case of certain common law jurisdictions, unlawfulness) towards legitimacy and acceptance in the international legal community. Litigation funding as we know it today first gained traction in Australia in the 1990s and has since developed quickly, especially in other common law jurisdictions such as the United Kingdom and the United States. The starting point has generally been those particular areas of dispute resolution where funding is most needed, such as insolvency litigation, investment treaty arbitration and class actions. Over time, however, funding has become increasingly established as a legitimate tool for the funding of commercial disputes generally. In a 2016 judgment of the Court of Appeal of England and Wales, it was described as "an accepted and judicially sanctioned activity perceived to be in the public interest".[1]

At present, the industry remains largely unregulated, although given the flood of capital that has surged into the market over recent years, it is perhaps unsurprising that there have been calls for increased regulatory controls. Responses to the issue of regulation internationally have been mixed. In Australia, for example, following the introduction of regulations in 2020, funders of class actions were treated as fund managers and subjected to a number of additional regulatory hurdles, only for the new Labor government to announce just two years later that those requirements would be scaled back significantly. Meanwhile, on 13 September 2022, the European Parliament voted in favour of new rules to strengthen the regulation of the EU litigation funding sector proposed by German Member of the European Parliament Axel Voss. However, criticisms were voiced by the International Legal Finance Association (ILFA),[2] a global independent association of commercial third-party funders, and it now appears that there will be a delay to the implementation of these regulations pending a proposed 'mapping study' of the litigation funding landscape by the European Commission. In Germany, legislation came into force in October 2023 implementing the EU Representative Actions Directive (EU) 2020/1828 and allowing for the first time consumer class actions pursuing payments against companies, but at the same time limiting the third-party funder's economic share in any proceeds to 10% – a restriction that could severely hamper the availability of funding for such claims.

From a public policy perspective, those in favour of regulation highlight the need to protect consumers from the risk of abuses in the market such as excessive profiteering and improper third-party control over disputes. Conversely, there is the risk of stifling the funding market

From a public policy perspective, those in favour of regulation highlight the need to protect consumers from the risk of abuses in the market such as excessive profiteering and improper third-party control over disputes.

through enhanced protections and thereby inadvertently hindering access to justice. After all, as observed in a judgment of the UK Competition Appeal Tribunal (CAT), litigation funding is seen as "a well-recognised feature of modern litigation [that] facilitates access to justice for those who otherwise may be unable to afford it".[3]

In this chapter, we focus on the regulatory position in England and Wales, which today is considered to be one of the most developed and sophisticated global centres for third-party funding.

2. Background

In the absence of any specific statutory regulatory framework, the legal position in respect of third-party funding in England and Wales has developed mostly by reference to case law. Historically, litigation funding arrangements could constitute both a crime and a tort, and were treated as void and unenforceable as a matter of public policy under the English law doctrines of maintenance of champerty. However, as third-party funding is increasingly seen as an important (and timely) driver of access to justice, the law has developed in such a way that, today, a typical litigation funding agreement (LFA) with a professional funder will generally not fall foul of these rules unless it involves some particular element of impropriety, such as an ability for the funder to exert excessive control over the proceedings or something that otherwise tends to "undermine the ends of justice".[4] In particular, the Court of Appeal has confirmed that "rigorous analysis of law, facts and witnesses, consideration of proportionality and review at appropriate intervals" is to be expected of a responsible funder and cannot of itself be champertous.[5]

An important milestone in the growth of the industry came with the publication in January 2010 of the so-called Jackson Report, which followed Sir Rupert Jackson's review of civil litigation costs in England and Wales and gave credence to third-party funding by identifying a number of benefits.[6] At the time, Jackson did not consider that full regulation of the industry was required, but instead recommended that a voluntary code for litigation funders be drawn up containing appropriate protections. He suggested that consideration should be given to statutory regulation in future depending on how the industry developed.

3. Self-regulation

In response to the Jackson Report, an independent body called the Association of Litigation Funders (ALF) was established with a mandate to facilitate the self-regulation of the funding market in England and Wales in line with a Code of Conduct. The code was first published in November 2011 by the Civil Justice Council, an agency of the Ministry of Justice, and has subsequently been updated on a number of occasions. Among other things, the code:

- requires funders to maintain adequate financial resources to meet their funding obligations;
- provides that funders must behave reasonably in relation to termination of LFAs and approval of settlements, with withdrawal of funding being permitted only in specific circumstances; and
- prevents funders from:
  - taking control of litigation or settlement negotiations; or
  - causing the claimant's lawyers to act in breach of their professional duties.

Although the code is voluntary, compliance is mandatory for the 15 currently subscribing funder members of the ALF.[7] As observed in a judgment of the CAT:

> *[The code] is a voluntary code and not a binding legal obligation, but we think that it is wholly unrealistic to suppose that a leading litigation funder that is commercially active in this field would not honour these commitments to the [ALF] of which it is a founder member, and thus place at risk the whole regime of self-regulation.*[8]

In theory, the scope of the code is limited to English court litigation; however, it is likely in practice that ALF members (and indeed many reputable non-members) will comply with the provisions of the code for all of their investments, including arbitration.

Jackson has since revisited the reforms made following the Jackson Report and suggested in March 2018 that his proposals to promote third-party funding and introduce the code had been successful:

> *These reforms enable parties to pursue claims (and sometimes defences) when they could not otherwise afford to do so. Funders are highly experienced litigators and they exercise effective control over costs. They often insist upon having court-approved budgets. Self-evidently, these reforms promote access to justice and tend to control costs.*[9]

It is worth noting that although the core business of litigation funding is not formally regulated, certain litigation funders are authorised by the Financial Conduct Authority (FCA) as investment managers and/or may be subject to additional oversight if, for example, they are a publicly listed company.

4. Judicial oversight

Inevitably, a degree of supervision over third-party funding arrangements is exerted by the courts and tribunals hearing funded cases. The English judiciary has generally demonstrated a 'pro-funding' attitude, with a number of civil court judgments endorsing the use of third-party funding and providing guidance on key issues impacting funded cases. For example, there is a long line of authorities relating to the so-called '*Arkin* cap' which, as long as the LFA was not champertous, limited a funder's potential liability for adverse costs to the amount of its investment.[10] The relevance of the *Arkin* cap, however, has been gradually diminished by a number of subsequent judgments, following which it is now clear that the courts retain a broad discretion as to costs and will not apply the cap automatically.[11] The courts have also considered the impact of a funder's involvement in a case in the context of security for costs, with the Court of Appeal observing that while the code is "not a very long or detailed document" under which members accept obligations – albeit only to the ALF – in relation to capital adequacy, ultimately:

> *a properly run commercial funder should rarely if ever need to be ordered to put up security. A funder should be structured, and operated, in such a way that there is little doubt that it will be able to satisfy any adverse costs order which may be made against it.*[12]

Funding has also been dealt with in a number of judgments of the CAT, where – due to the need to ensure the sufficiency of third-party funding and to protect the interests of class members that may not be participating in the proceedings – there is a greater level of oversight over funding arrangements at the stages of class certification and (at least in theory) settlement approval. That said, there has been a clear acknowledgement by the CAT that, without funding, the potentially very valuable claims on behalf of large numbers of aggrieved consumers that are often brought in the CAT – the sorts of claims which help to ensure that corporate wrongdoers modify their behaviour – would never be able to be brought.[13] While the CAT has to date taken a broadly permissive approach to funding arrangements at the certification stage, its stance in respect of settlements and the associated commercial considerations is yet to be tested.

5. Arbitration

There has been a significant increase in the use of third-party funding in international arbitration in recent years, with major arbitral centres such as Singapore and Hong Kong being the latest examples of jurisdictions (where funding remains at present generally impermissible for domestic proceedings) incrementally phasing in the legitimate use of funding in the international arbitration context first.[14] While there is no formal regulation of the use of third-party funding in arbitration which applies internationally, the increasing uptake of funding in the arbitration community generally is reflected by its treatment in:

- comprehensive studies such as the *Report of the ICCA-Queen Mary Task Force on Third-Party Funding in International Arbitration* (April 2018); and
- guidelines such as the International Bar Association's revised Guidelines on Conflicts of Interest in International Arbitration 2014.

In addition, a number of the major global arbitral institutions (including the Singapore International Arbitration Centre, the Hong Kong International Arbitration Centre, the Stockholm Chamber of Commerce Arbitration Institute, the International Chamber of Commerce and the International Centre for Settlement of Investment Disputes) have recently updated their respective rules to cover the issues that commonly arise in funded arbitrations, such as conflicts of interest, privilege and costs. Most of all, funded claimants are increasingly being required (either by the relevant rules or by order of the tribunal) to disclose to the respondent whether funding is in place and if so, the identity of the funder. It is less common for the disclosure of the funding terms to be required.

6. Solicitors' professional and ethical obligations

While third-party funding may not be subject to specific regulation *per se*, the solicitors who act for claimants in relation to funded cases (and indeed the many practising solicitors who are employed by litigation funders) are regulated by the Solicitors Regulatory Authority (SRA). The SRA's Code of Conduct contains a number of relevant provisions which will apply to firms and solicitors acting in the litigation funding context, including in relation to managing conflicts of interest, the duty of confidentiality and privilege.[15] This Code of Conduct also requires solicitors to provide their clients with the information they need to make informed decisions about the available funding options, including litigation funding and litigation risk insurance.

7. Contingency fee arrangements

Contingency fee arrangements between lawyers and their clients, whereby some or all of the lawyer's remuneration depends on the outcome of the case, are ultimately a form of risk sharing akin to third-party funding. Much like litigation funding, contingency fee arrangements were historically unlawful in England and Wales.

Statutory provision for conditional fee agreements (CFAs), whereby the client pays different amounts depending on the outcome of the case, was made pursuant to Section 58 of the Courts and Legal Services Act 1990. CFAs may provide for a 'success fee' payable in addition to non-conditional fees if a successful result is achieved in the dispute. The success fee is calculated as a percentage uplift on the lawyer's normal rates and, in commercial cases, the maximum uplift is 100%.

Contingency fee arrangements between lawyers and their clients, whereby some or all of the lawyer's remuneration depends on the outcome of the case, are ultimately a form of risk sharing akin to third-party funding.

Further, in another of the suite of reforms carried out following the Jackson Report, statutory provision was made for damages-based agreements (DBAs) in the context of most civil litigation pursuant to Section 45 of the Legal Aid, Sentencing and Punishment of Offenders Act 2012. DBAs are effectively a 'no win, no fee' agreement whereby the lawyer's remuneration is determined as a percentage of any damages recovered from the opponent. For general commercial claims (not including appeal proceedings), the 'DBA fee' (which will also cover counsel fees and value-added tax) is capped at 50% of the sum recovered under the Damages-Based Agreements Regulations 2013 ('DBA Regulations'), which provide various additional requirements for DBAs. Importantly, pursuant to Section 58AA of the Courts and Legal Services Act 1990, a DBA is unenforceable if it does not satisfy the relevant statutory conditions.

8. *PACCAR*: LFAs as DBAs

Until recently, there was a general understanding among stakeholders in the litigation funding market that English law did not treat LFAs as DBAs, and that they thus were not subject to the applicable legal regime. However, in a July 2023 judgment in which the Supreme Court interpreted the relevant statutory provisions relating to DBAs, this general consensus was subverted.[16] In *PACCAR*, the Supreme Court held that third-party funders are 'persons providing claims management services' under the proper interpretation of Section 58AA of the Courts and Legal Services Act 1990. As a result, as things presently stand, LFAs where the return to the funder is calculated by reference to the damages recovered must comply with the DBA Regulations. Crucially, if such an LFA does not comply with the DBA Regulations, it will be unenforceable. It was conceded in *PACCAR* that the relevant LFA would be rendered unenforceable by this finding, alongside potentially many other existing English law-governed LFAs.

At the time of writing, the precise scope of the *PACCAR* judgment remains unclear and stakeholders, as well as the court system, are continuing to digest its implications. In January 2024, Justice Secretary Alex Chalk was reported as stating that "the government will be reversing the damaging effects of PACCAR at the first legislative opportunity". Pending any legislative 'solution' to this issue, which is currently being debated in government in the context of proposed amendments to the Digital Markets and Consumers Bill, it now appears (at least as a matter of English law) that litigation funders must choose between either:

- a 'damages-based' pricing structure which is compliant with the DBA Regulations; or
- a 'non-damages-based' structure which should fall outside the scope of the DBA Regulations.

In the context of opt-out group claims in the CAT, the position is different, as DBAs are expressly unenforceable under Section 47C(8) of the Competition Act 1998, meaning that the option of adopting a damages-based pricing structure is not currently available. In the wake of *PACCAR*, funders across the market have assessed their existing LFAs with a view to amending or reissuing those that may be impacted so as to minimise the risk of potentially damaging enforceability arguments being raised in future, either by the defendant in the dispute or even by an opportunistic claimant seeking to avoid payment of the funder's fee.

9. Litigation risk insurance

Another form of risk sharing in relation to disputes is litigation risk insurance, which is a form of after-the-event legal expenses insurance. Although various types of litigation risk insurance are available, the most common in the context of third-party funding is adverse costs insurance, which covers the insured and/or the funder for the opponent's legal costs in the event that the litigation or arbitration is unsuccessful. Both insurers and insurance brokers are regulated by the FCA and must comply with a variety of applicable laws and regulations.

Notes

1 *Excalibur Ventures LLC v Texas Keystone Inc (No 2)* [2016] EWCA Civ 1144 at [31].
2 See ILFA, *Resourcing the Rule of Law in Europe* (June 2023).
3 *UK Trucks Claim Limited v Fiat Chrysler Automobiles NV* and *Road Haulage Association Limited v Man SE* [2019] CAT 26 at [17].
4 *Factortame (No 8)* [2002] EWCA Civ 932 at [36].
5 *Excalibur Ventures LLC v Texas Keystone Inc* [2016] EWCA Civ 1144.
6 Sir Rupert Jackson, *Review of Civil Litigation Costs: Final Report* (2009), Chapter 11.
7 Several UK funders are also members of the ILFA, which was founded in 2020 and has its own best practices.
8 *UK Trucks Claim Limited v Fiat Chrysler Automobiles NV* and *Road Haulage Association Limited v Man SE* [2019] CAT 26 at [54].
9 "Was It All Worth It?", lecture by Sir Rupert Jackson to the Cambridge Law Faculty, 5 March 2018.
10 *Arkin v Borchard Lines Ltd* [2005] EWCA Civ 655; *Excalibur Ventures LLC v Texas Keystone Inc* [2016] EWCA Civ 1144.
11 See, eg, *Bailey v Glaxosmithkline UK Ltd* [2017] EWHC 3195 (QB); *Davey v Money* [2019] EWHC 997 (Ch); *Chapelgate Credit Opportunity Master Fund Ltd v Money* [2020] EWCA Civ 246; and *Laser Trust v CFL Finance Ltd* [2021] EWHC 1404 (Ch).
12 *Rowe v Ingenious Media Holdings plc* [2021] EWCA Civ 29 at [78].
13 See, eg, *Mark McLaren v MOL* [2022] CAT 10 at [148].
14 See, in relation to Singapore, the Singapore Civil Law (Amendment) Bill 2016 and Civil Law (Third-Party Funding) Regulations 2016; and in relation to Hong Kong, the Arbitration and Mediation Legislation (Third Party Funding) (Amendment) Ordinance 2017 and the Code of Practice for Third-Party Funding of Arbitration issued by the Hong Kong Department of Justice.
15 Similar principles apply to barristers under the Code of Conduct of the Bar.
16 *R (on the application of PACCAR Inc) v Competition Appeal Tribunal* [2023] UKSC 28.

V. Legal barriers to funding

Moeiz Farhan
Vasanti Selvaratnam KC
36 Stone

1. Introduction

The purpose of this chapter is to outline the extent to which English law has – and has not – moved on from the common law's historic hostility to arrangements by which third parties finance litigation between others. That hostility has traditionally been reflected in the doctrines of champerty and maintenance but continues to colour – through considerations of public policy – the extent to which different types of litigation funding arrangements are enforceable under English law.

2. Historic background: maintenance and champerty

In this context, 'maintenance' refers to the support by a stranger of litigation in which it has no legitimate concern without just cause or excuse.[1] 'Champerty' is an aggravated form of maintenance and refers to the support of litigation by a stranger in return for a share of the proceeds.[2] The origin of maintenance and champerty as crimes and torts is medieval. In *Giles v Thompson*, Lord Mustill remarked:[3]

> *the crimes of maintenance and champerty are so old that their origins can no longer be traced, but their importance in medieval times is quite clear. The mechanisms of justice lacked the internal strength to resist the oppression of private individuals through suits fomented and sustained by unscrupulous men of power. Champerty was particularly vicious, since the purchase of a share in litigation*

> *presented an obvious temptation to the suborning of justices and witnesses and the exploitation of worthless claims which the defendant lacked the resources and influence to withstand. The fact that such conduct was treated as both criminal and tortious provided an invaluable external discipline to which, as the records show, recourse was often required.*

In 1967, Parliament abolished the crimes and torts of maintenance and champerty by Sections 13 and 14 of the Criminal Law Act 1967. However, Section 14(2) of the 1967 act provided that such abolition "shall not affect any rule of [the law of England and Wales] as to cases in which a contract is to be treated as contrary to public policy or otherwise illegal". The consequence of that proviso is that, although maintenance and champerty no longer constitute crimes or torts, they are capable as a rule of public policy of rendering unenforceable contracts that fall foul of those doctrines.

In the modern law, a contract will be considered a contract of maintenance (and therefore unenforceable) where all aspects of the transaction taken together constitute "wanton and officious intermeddling with the disputes of others where the meddler has no interest whatever, and where the assistance he renders to one or the other party is without justification or excuse".[4] What constitutes sufficient 'justification or excuse' for this purpose has significantly widened over time. In large part, this reflects a changing attitude towards litigation funding and related arrangements as a necessary means of ensuring access to justice.

What is clear, however, is that litigation funding will not *per se* amount to maintenance or champerty. In *Excalibur Ventures LLC v Texas Keystone Inc*,[5] the Court of Appeal described litigation funding as "an accepted and judicially sanctioned activity perceived to be in the public interest". More recently, in the *Akhmedova* litigation, Justice Knowles said that it was "difficult to envisage how litigation funding conducted by a responsible funder adhering to the Code of Conduct could be construed to be illegal and offensive champerty or might be held to corrupt justice".[6] There might, of course, be exceptional cases where a funding agreement purports to give a funder undue control over the conduct of the dispute, but the boundaries of what is acceptable will be for the courts to determine on a case-by-case basis.

In addition, Parliament has introduced a statutory framework to permit certain fee arrangements (eg, conditional fee agreements (CFAs) and damages-based agreements (DBAs)) that would otherwise be unenforceable at common law. This is discussed further below. Outside this statutory framework the common law continues to apply, although its scope is more limited than in the past.

3. The current position

The different types of funding arrangements that are now typically available have been described in detail elsewhere in this text. For present purposes, we set out below a brief summary of the different arrangements that are typically available and the relevant legal framework that applies.

3.1 Conditional fee agreements

CFAs (not to be confused with 'contingency fee agreements', which in England are known as DBAs) are governed by Sections 58 and 58A of the Courts and Legal Services Act 1990. A CFA is a type of contractual arrangement whereby the legal fees (or any part of them) of a person providing advocacy or litigation services are payable only in specific circumstances (usually, 'success' in the litigation).

Section 58(1) of the 1990 act provides that:

- a CFA which satisfies all the statutory conditions shall not be unenforceable only by reason of it being a CFA; and
- any other CFA shall not be enforceable.

Thus, the statute:

- provides a statutory bar against compliant CFAs being rendered unenforceable on grounds of public policy (ie, on the basis that it infringed the doctrines of maintenance and champerty); and
- renders unenforceable all other CFAs.

Under a typical CFA, a lawyer agrees an hourly fee with the client, which the lawyer agrees to forgo if the client is unsuccessful. At the same time, it is agreed that if the client is successful, the lawyer will recover their base fee (ie, the total hourly fees chargeable) plus a success fee calculated as a percentage of the base fee. The definition of 'success' for these purposes is a matter of contractual negotiation and might typically be defined by reference to:

- a particular result in the litigation (eg, a positive finding of liability); or
- the quantum of damages awarded or recovered on enforcement.

As originally enacted, Section 58 of the 1990 act provided that the statutory bar would extend only to CFAs in 'specific proceedings' – that is, proceedings designated by the lord chancellor by statutory instrument. Section 58 was 'activated' for the first time in 1995 when the lord chancellor made the Conditional Fee Agreements Order 1995 (SI 1995/1674) specifying three types of permitted proceedings –

namely personal injury, insolvency and European Convention on Human Rights applications. Article 3 of that order provided that the maximum increase on the normal level of fees that a lawyer could claim in a successful case was 100%. In 1998, the 1995 order was revoked and CFAs became permissible in all proceedings (save criminal and certain family proceedings). The maximum permitted percentage increase remained 100%.

In 1999, Parliament passed the Access to Justice Act 1999. This replaced the original Section 58 in the 1990 act with a new Section 58 and Section 58A. Among other things, the effect of these new provisions was to provide that both the base fee and the success fee under a CFA and after-the-event (ATE) premiums (as to which see below) could be recoverable from the losing party as costs in civil litigation. This remained the position until 2013 when, following Lord Justice Jackson's Review of Civil Litigation Costs, the 1990 act was amended by the Legal Aid, Sentencing and Punishment of Offenders Act 2012 so as to abolish (with some exceptions and transitional provisions) the recovery of CFA success fees and ATE premiums.

In order to be compliant with the statutory conditions set forth in Section 58 of the 1990 act, a CFA must be an agreement for 'advocacy or litigation services'. One issue that has arisen in this context is whether an agreement in respect of pre-action conduct can constitute a CFA. The definition of 'litigation services' in Section 119 of the 1990 act, read together with Section 58A(4), requires the services to have been provided in respect of proceedings that have commenced or are contemplated. In *Gaynor v Central West London Buses Ltd,*[7] the Court of Appeal held that this meant that a retainer letter that stated that no charge would be made for pre-litigation services if the opponent disputed the claim and the client decided not to pursue it was not a CFA and was therefore not unenforceable for failure to comply with the statutory requirements, because "until the potential defendant disputes the claim, it is not possible to say that proceedings are contemplated".[8]

Nonetheless, the definition of a 'CFA' is broad enough to encompass different types of agreements. It is possible to have a CFA which does not provide for a success fee at all. In such a case, a lawyer agrees to forgo all of their fees if the client loses but will recover their ordinary costs in the event of success. It is also possible to have CFAs which provide for discounted hourly rates to apply whatever the outcome of the proceedings, with success in the claim triggering the lawyer's entitlement to the balance of the base costs and possibly also a success fee.

It is possible to have a CFA which does not provide for a success fee at all. In such a case, a lawyer agrees to forgo all of their fees if the client loses but will recover their ordinary costs in the event of success.

3.2 Damages-based agreements

Statutory provision was first made for DBAs with the passage of the Coroners and Justice Act 2009, Section 154 of which inserted a new Section 58AA into the Courts and Legal Services Act 1990. As originally enacted, Section 58AA only made provision for DBAs in employment claims. That limitation was removed with effect from 19 January 2013 by Section 45 of the Legal Aid, Sentencing and Punishment of Offenders Act 2012.

As defined in Section 58AA(3), a DBA is an agreement between a person providing advocacy services, litigation services or claims management services and the recipient of those services which provides that:

- the recipient is to make a payment to the person providing the services if the recipient obtains a specified financial benefit in connection with the matter in relation to which the services are provided; and
- the amount of that payment is to be determined by reference to the amount of the financial benefit obtained.

Payment under a DBA is often (but not always) calculated as a percentage of the damages awarded to the claimant.

In order to constitute a valid DBA, an agreement must comply with the terms of Section 58AA and the additional detailed requirements contained in the Damages-Based Agreement Regulations 2013 (SI 2013/609). In particular, the agreement:

- must be in writing;
- must not relate to proceedings that cannot be the subject of an enforceable CFA under Section 58A;
- must not provide for payment above the prescribed amount; and
- must specify:
  - the claim or proceedings to which it relates;
  - the circumstances in which the lawyer's payment, expenses and costs will be payable; and
  - the reason for setting the amount of the payment at the level agreed.

In non-personal injury claims, a DBA must not provide for payment above 50% of the sums ultimately recovered by the client.[9] This limitation applies only to claims at first instance and not to appeals.[10] In addition, a DBA must not require any amount to be paid by a client other than the contingency fee itself and any expenses incurred by the legal representative, net of any amount which has been paid or is payable by another party to the proceedings.[11] Costs that are recovered from the other side go towards meeting the contingency fee.

3.3 Insurance

It is perfectly possible for a client which anticipates that it may in due course be involved in disputes or litigation to take out insurance in respect of future legal expenses. This is known as 'before-the-event' (BTE) insurance, since it is taken out before the 'event' which gives rise to the litigation in question. Writing in 2009, Lord Justice Jackson noted as part of his Review of Civil Litigation Costs that while larger enterprises often take out employer's liability insurance, public liability insurance and (where relevant) professional indemnity insurance, they rarely tend to take out BTE insurance, preferring to meet the costs of disputes and consequential litigation as and when they arise. However, he noted that small and medium-sized enterprises often do take out such cover (usually sold as commercial legal expenses insurance), but this cover usually excludes contractual disputes arising in the course of business.[12]

An alternative product is ATE insurance, which covers a litigant against any future liability for the costs of an opposing party. It is taken out after the 'event' which has given rise to the dispute and the consequential costs risk. Some ATE policies will also provide cover against the client's own costs and disbursements.

ATE insurance is often taken out by clients that are represented under a CFA or DBA because, while they may not be liable to pay their own lawyer's fees if they are unsuccessful, they may still be liable for the other side's costs. ATE insurance mitigates this adverse costs risk. However, as noted above, since 2013, ATE insurance premiums are not recoverable as costs by a successful party.

3.4 Third-party funding

'Third-party funding' (or 'litigation funding') usually refers to an agreement whereby a non-party – the funder – agrees to provide a claimant with funds to meet the expenses of taking legal proceedings. In exchange, the funder takes a share of the proceeds of a successful claim. Where third-party funding is combined with a CFA or a DBA, it may be the case that only part of the legal fees is funded by a third party, with the balance funded by a law firm acting under a CFA or DBA.

Lawyers properly acting under CFAs or DBAs will not usually be liable for the costs of their clients' opponents.[13] However, the position is different where the litigation is funded by a professional funder. In *Arkin v Borchard Lines Ltd*,[14] the Court of Appeal held that a professional funder that finances part of a claimant's costs of litigation

ATE insurance is often taken out by clients that are represented under a CFA or DBA because, while they may not be liable to pay their own lawyer's fees if they are unsuccessful, they may still be liable for the other side's costs.

should be potentially liable for the costs of the opposing party to the extent of the funding provided. This liability is potentially justifiable on at least two grounds:

- It is the funder's support which has allowed the ultimately unmeritorious claim to be pursued (and costs to be incurred); and
- The funder can in some cases be described as the 'real' party to the litigation since it stands to benefit financially from success.

This cap on a funder's liability – to the extent of the funding provided – is often described as the '*Arkin*' cap after the case from which it emerged. But it is not a rule of law and the view of the courts has to some extent moved on. Importantly, since *Arkin* was decided in 2005, the availability of commercial funding has increased dramatically and third-party funding of commercial cases has become much more common. The court's unfettered discretion as to costs was reaffirmed in *Davey v Money*,[15] in which the Court of Appeal dismissed an appeal by a commercial funder against an order holding it liable for all of the respondents' costs from the date of the underlying funding agreement. Lord Justice Newey observed:

> *I do not consider that the Arkin approach represents a binding rule. Judges, as it seems to me, retain a discretion and, depending on the facts, may consider it appropriate to take into account matters other than the extent of the funder's funding and not to limit the funder's liability to the amount of that funding. In the case of a funder who funded only a distinct part of a claimant's costs, a judge might well decide that it should pay no larger sum towards the defendant's costs. A judge could also, however, consider the funder's potential return significant. The more a funder had stood to gain, the closer he might be thought to be to the "real party" ordinarily ordered to pay the successful party's costs ... In the case of a funder who had funded the lion's share of a claimant's costs in return for the lion's share of the potential fruits of litigation against multiple parties, it would not be surprising if the judge ordered the funder to bear at least the lion's share of the winners' costs, regardless of whether the funder's outlay on the claimant's costs had been a lesser figure.*[16]

One of the consequences of the decision in *Davey* is that commercial funders are likely to insist upon:

- sufficient ATE insurance being purchased to cover their adverse costs risk; or
- a larger share of the proceeds of any eventual judgment to compensate them for this risk.

Until very recently, it was assumed that litigation funding agreements – where a funder plays no active role in the conduct of the litigation but is entitled to be remunerated based on a percentage of damages recovered – would not constitute a DBA, and that therefore there was no need to comply with the DBA Regulations. Indeed, the longstanding position in England has been that the litigation funding market is self-regulated (by bodies such as the Association of Litigation Funders (ALF)). In 2017, in response to a written question to the Ministry of Justice, the government stated that it "does not believe that the case has been made out for moving away for voluntary regulation".[17]

That assumption has proved incorrect. In *R (on the application of PACCAR Inc) v Competition Appeal Tribunal*,[18] the Supreme Court held that funding under such an agreement constituted the provision of a 'claim management service' and therefore such litigation funding agreements must comply with the regulatory regime for DBAs; otherwise, they will be unenforceable. In her dissenting judgment, Lady Rose quoted the chair of the ALF:

> *These consequences [ie, that funders cannot enforce their agreement for the repayment of the millions of pounds they have spent] will extend to all or most litigation funding agreements that have been agreed since litigation funding began in England and Wales. This would be massively damaging both for the administration of justice in relation to the existing cases which involve funding by litigation funders, and the future access to justice of parties who would otherwise have employed litigation funding agreements to fund their cases. It would bring to an abrupt end hundreds of funded claims with potentially catastrophic financial consequences for all involved in the case. It would have a major impact on the development of group litigations before the English Courts (including but not limited to Collective Proceedings Orders before the Competition Appeals Tribunal), given the inter-relationship between that group litigation and the litigation funding industry. This would have enormous financial consequences: there is estimated to be over £500 million of costs incurred annually by litigation funders in the UK alone. It would also have huge policy implications for the litigation funding industry, which ALF is best-placed to address.*[19]

The fallout from *PACCAR* was particularly acute in the context of opt-out collective proceedings in the Competition Appeal Tribunal (CAT), where DBAs are prohibited. On 15 November 2023, the government responded by tabling an amendment to the Digital Markets, Competition and Consumers Bill which would have had the effect of removing this prohibition for DBAs with funders (but not with solicitors or barristers). However, that amendment would not have removed the need for the DBAs in question to comply with the DBA Regulations.

At the time of writing, the government has just announced a more fundamental legislative amendment in the form of the Litigation Funding Agreements (Enforceability) Bill, to remove litigation funding agreements from the scope of the DBA Regulations entirely. The bill provides that the amendment is to be treated as always having had effect.

In the meantime, it is apparent that funders are moving quickly to avoid the consequences of *PACCAR* by amending their funding models and, where necessary, renegotiating existing agreements. These attempts were tested in a recent case, *Commercial and Interregional Card Claims I Ltd v Mastercard Incorporated*,[20] in which the CAT confirmed that a litigation funding agreement in which a funder's fee was based on a multiple of the funding provided rather than a share of damages recovered was not a DBA for the purposes of the DBA Regulations (even if capped by reference to the amount of those damages). That case is subject to appeal.

4. The international perspective

The discussion so far has focused on the position in England as it typically applies to civil litigation in the English courts. The sorts of funding arrangements discussed in this chapter are also often employed in international disputes – principally those that the parties have agreed are to be resolved by way of international arbitration.

The extent to which third-party funding and models such as CFAs and DBAs are employed in international arbitration is clear due to the inherently confidential nature of most international arbitrations. One of the more comprehensive studies is the *Report of the ICCA-Queen Mary Task Force on Third-Party Funding in International Arbitration*, published in April 2018.[21] That report observed an "upsurge" in the number of law firms working with third-party funders and the number of reported cases involving issues relating to funding.

Where the relevant arrangements are expressly made subject to English law by way of a governing law clause, it is likely that the common law and statutory framework discussed thus far will apply with full force to the funding of international arbitrations, even where the arbitration is to take place outside of England and the law of the seat, the law governing the substance of the dispute and the law of the arbitration agreement are all other than English law. This is likely to be a common situation where the law firms or litigation funders involved are based in England.

The extent to which third-party funding and models such as CFAs and DBAs are employed in international arbitration is clear due to the inherently confidential nature of most international arbitrations.

The availability of CFAs and DBAs in international arbitration is expressly provided for by statute. Section 58A(4) of the Courts and Legal Services Act 1990 provides (in relation to CFAs) that CFAs are available in respect of 'proceedings', to include "any sort of proceedings for resolving disputes (and not just proceedings in a court), whether commenced or contemplated". A similar provision appears in Section 58AA(7A) in relation to DBAs. The application of these provisions will be straightforward where the relevant agreements are (or purport to be) governed by English law; but in other cases, there may be disputes about the territorial scope of the English statutes. In practice, one might expect the agreements to be governed by the law of the relevant lawyers' home state, which in turn will contain its own provisions governing the use of CFAs and DBAs by lawyers in that jurisdiction.

The rules against maintenance and champerty also extend to arbitration (*Bevan Ashford v Geoff Yeandle*),[22] and so will have an impact on the outer limits of what is an acceptable third-party funding agreement in that context as regards funding agreements governed by English law. However, the fact that lawyers in international arbitrations are often qualified in different jurisdictions (which may or may not have their own professional conduct rules in relation to third-party funding) means that there is the possibility of additional layers of complexity.

Notes

1 *Chitty on Contracts*, 35th edition (Sweet and Maxwell, 2023) at §19–147.
2 *Giles v Thompson* [1993] 3 All ER 321 at 328 (CA). See also *Re Trepca Mines Ltd (No 2)* [1963] Ch 199 at 224; *Trendtex Trading Corp v Credit Suisse* [1980] 1 QB 629 at 663.
3 *Giles v Thompson* [1994] 1 AC 142 at 153.
4 *Ibid* at 164.
5 *Excalibur Ventures LLC v Texas Keystone Inc* [2016] EWCA Civ 1144.
6 *Akhmedova v Akhmedov* [2020] EWHC 1526 (Fam) at § 45.
7 *Gaynor v Central West London Buses Ltd* [2006] EWCA Civ 1120.
8 *Ibid* at § 17.
9 Damages-Based Agreement Regulations 2013, r 4(3).
10 *Ibid*, r 4(4).
11 *Ibid*, r 4(1).
12 *Review of Civil Litigation Costs: Preliminary Report* (May 2009) at pp152–153.
13 This has been expressly held in relation to CFAs (*Hodgson v Imperial Tobacco Ltd* [1998] EWCA Civ 224) and is assumed to be the case in relation to solicitors acting under DBAs. However, they may be liable if they go beyond the scope of a solicitor's ordinary role and act as a funder of litigation: *Germany v Flatman* [2011] EWHC 2945 (QB).
14 *Arkin v Borchard Lines Ltd* [2005] EWCA Civ 655.
15 *Davey v Money* [2020] EWCA Civ 246.
16 *Ibid* at [38].
17 Written question – HL4216 (24 January 2017).
18 *R (on the application of PACCAR Inc) v Competition Appeal Tribunal* [2023] UKSC 28.
19 [2023] UKSC 28] at § 243.
20 [2024] CAT 3.
21 https://cdn.arbitration-icca.org/s3fs-public/document/media_document/Third-Party-Funding-Report%20.pdf.
22 *Bevan Ashford v Geoff Yeandle* [1998] 3 WLR 172.

VI. Disclosure of information

Ewelina Kajkowska
Hogan Lovells International LLP
David J Kerstein
Arcadia Finance LLC
Nicole Silver
Ignite Specialty Risk

1. Confidentiality and privilege

In cases involving third-party funding, an issue of confidentiality and privilege arises throughout the arbitration. A funder will require access to privileged documents and information to make an informed decision about the merits and associated risks of the case to determine the prospects for success and decide whether and on what basis to provide funding. The provision to a funder of any documents may result in the potential waiver of privilege and confidentiality, meaning that such information could become subject to disclosure requests by the opponent in the arbitration. Such an outcome has the potential to compromise the core principle of confidentiality – a factor that not only underpins the relationship between lawyer and client, but also frequently draws parties to prefer arbitration over litigation as a method of dispute resolution.

In light of the above, protection of confidentiality and privilege is essential in a third-party funding scenario. This, however, poses significant challenges, particularly in an international setting. First, the doctrines of confidentiality and privilege vary across jurisdictions, frequently leading to inconsistent standards. Second, various rules and laws might be relevant to determine issues of privilege,[1] and often a complex conflict of laws analysis is required to determine the existence and scope of any privilege. Finally, the concept of third-party funding is still developing in the jurisprudence of different countries. As a result, there is limited guidance and case law on how issues of privilege will be determined.

1.1 What kind of privilege?

The type of privilege afforded to information and documents depends on the jurisdiction. In England, the relevant heads of privilege are twofold:

- legal advice privilege (lawyer to client); and
- litigation privilege (legal work product).

Legal advice privilege protects confidential communications between legal counsel and a client made for the purpose of seeking and receiving legal advice. Litigation privilege is used to protect communications whose dominant purpose is to aid pending or contemplated litigation. Importantly, litigation privilege extends beyond protecting communications merely between a client and lawyer, and also includes communications with a third party. It can therefore be argued that litigation privilege may apply to communications with third-party funders.

Legal advice privilege protects confidential communications between legal counsel and a client made for the purpose of seeking and receiving legal advice.

Additionally, the concept of common interest might apply to permit the disclosure of privileged documents to a third party with a common interest in the arbitration concerned, including a third-party funder.

1.2 What is the scope of privilege?

In the absence of a prior agreement between the parties, and subject to its underlying obligation to act fairly and impartially, an arbitral tribunal:

- is not required under national arbitration laws or institutional rules to determine privilege in any particular way; and
- has discretion to decide whether a particular piece of evidence should be produced or admitted to the record in the proceedings.

In the absence of consolidated guidance, arbitrators will frequently turn to the principle of *lex arbitri* – the law of the country where disclosure is sought or the law governing the arbitration agreement – to address issues of privilege.

Under English law, there is limited case law on the application of common interest or litigation privilege in the context of third-party funding. Some guidance as to the scope of application of common interest privilege follows from the decision in *Winterthur Swiss Insurance Company v AG (Manchester) Ltd*.[2] The case considered the situations in which common interest privilege might apply in the context of an insured providing documents to an insurer. It was confirmed that there are no situations in which there would definitely be a common interest; instead, each situation must be judged on the merits of its own facts. It could be argued that, by analogy with an insurer, a third-party funder may be deemed to share a common interest in the confidentiality of communications with the party's lawyer on the basis of a common interest in pursuing arbitration.

The existence of legal advice privilege in a third-party funding scenario was confirmed in *Edwardian Group Ltd v Singh*.[3] In this case, the court refused an application for an order for the inspection of the party's funding documents, holding that a funding agreement was subject to legal advice privilege.

1.3 Protecting privilege

Where a high level of confidentiality is required and commercially sensitive information is involved, parties will wish to initiate a discussion at the outset of the arbitration to ensure that confidentiality is preserved while permitting necessary disclosures to (multiple) funders.

Privilege can be protected by:

- disclosing the documents on the express basis that there is no intention to waive privilege; and
- obtaining an undertaking from the funder that it will keep the documents confidential.

Accordingly, a confidentiality or non-disclosure agreement is frequently entered into between the funder and the claim holder at the outset of an arbitration. Confidentiality provisions may also be inserted into the funding agreement itself.

Key terms that should be considered to protect confidentiality and privilege include:

- an assertion of the relevant privilege (including recording a common interest in the arbitration);
- a clear statement that no waiver of privilege is intended;
- the specification of the limited purpose for which information is being disclosed;
- an unequivocal undertaking to keep all information received confidential;
- the consequences of any unauthorised disclosure of information; and
- provisions for the return of information.

If the funded party and the funder enter into robust confidentiality arrangements, key documents disclosed to a funder may continue to attract litigation or common interest privilege. Importantly, however, mere labelling of the relevant communications may not suffice. In *AL v XYZ Ltd*,[4] the court emphasised that waiver of privilege is determined objectively: "If objectively, a client waives privilege it cannot then claim that the waiver did not exist simply because it (subjectively) asserts there has been no waiver." Care must therefore be taken to ensure not only that the safeguards above are put in place, but also that there has not in fact been a waiver of privilege, notwithstanding assertions to the contrary.

Separately, parties should also consider what material in fact needs to be shared. A balance must be struck between limiting risk and meeting the funder's need for adequate information both when considering whether to make an offer for funding and throughout the proceedings.

2. Conflicts of interest

Despite all the confusion, in practice, conflicts of interest rarely arise in the context of third-party funding. This is because a funder is never financing opposing parties in the same dispute. Moreover, no conflict

If the funded party and the funder enter into robust confidentiality arrangements, key documents disclosed to a funder may continue to attract litigation or common interest privilege.

will arise if a funder finances a dispute on behalf of client A against client B and later finances an unrelated dispute on behalf of client B against client C – or even client A. Of course, there may be business reasons why a funder would not want to finance an unrelated case brought by client B, particularly against client A; but no actual conflict will arise if the cases are unrelated and pursued at different times.[5]

Of course, there are exceptions to every rule. The exception most often discussed in the context of third-party funding and international arbitration is the potential for a conflict of interest to arise where there is a relationship between an arbitrator and a funder. Such a relationship could impact – theoretically at least – the impartiality and independence of the arbitrator, depending on the depth and breadth of the relationship and the arbitrator's awareness of the relationship. The primary concern is that an arbitrator may have a financial interest in, or some other connection with, the third-party funder that is financing a claimant which is appearing in a case before that arbitrator. This worry is similar to concerns about relationships between the arbitrator and the parties, their counsel or witnesses.

A second concern that can create a conflict of interest is involvement of the same funder in two cases with the same person acting in two different capacities (either arbitrator or counsel). It is thought that where an arbitrator is regularly appointed or seeks appointments from claimants in different arbitrations which are funded by the same funder, questions could arise as to the impartiality and independence of the arbitrator. Such risks are more pronounced in arbitration, since arbitrators are appointed *ad hoc* for each arbitration, often by the parties, and the same individuals may act alternately as arbitrator or counsel. It is for these reasons that disclosure by the funded party of the identity of the funder is now often encouraged, or in some cases required, by many arbitral institutions.

The 2014 International Bar Association (IBA) Guidelines on Conflicts of Interest in International Arbitration were the first regulatory instrument to extend conflict of interest rules in international arbitration to funders. Although not binding in the absence of an agreement by the parties, the IBA guidelines are increasingly seen as representing the international standard for determining conflicts of interest and the independence of an arbitrator. Certainly, the IBA guidelines are a useful tool for arbitrators and for arbitration practitioners to decide:

- whether circumstances exist "that would give rise to justifiable doubts as to the arbitrator's impartiality or independence"; and
- what sorts of conflicts (or the appearance thereof) should be disclosed.[6]

3. Disclosure of funding arrangements to other parties

As third-party funding becomes increasingly mainstream and more frequently used, many arbitral institutions are seeking to amend their rules to include requirements pertaining to disclosure and notice. The requirement for disclosure of third-party funding is largely premised on a desire to avoid a conflict of interest (eg, those described in the foregoing section) between the arbitrators and the funder.

3.1 Rules requiring mandatory disclosure of third-party funding

The latest and most robust provision to address third-party funding is Rule 14 of the 2022 International Centre for Settlement of Investment Disputes (ICSID) Rules,[7] which requires a party receiving funding to inform the secretary general – who in turn will notify the other party and the arbitrators – of the name and address of, and persons or entities that control or own, the funder. Rule 14(3) makes plain that the purpose of this rule is to avoid any conflict of interest, stating that notice should be given to "any arbitrator proposed for appointment or appointed in a proceeding *for purposes of completing the arbitrator declaration required by Rule 19(3)(b)*".[8]

While a tribunal could, in theory, order disclosure of further information regarding the funding agreement and/or the finance company providing the funding under Rule 14(4),[9] it is important to understand that such disclosure would (and should) be rare. This is because Rule 14 is not a disclosure, evidentiary or discovery rule;[10] rather, it is a procedural rule that is found in the chapter regarding the establishment of the tribunal. Thus, it is best understood as a rule aimed solely at helping the tribunal to determine (and avoid) conflicts. It is hard to imagine a scenario in which a claimant would need to provide to the institution or the tribunal other – often highly confidential – information, such as the terms of its agreement with its funder, so that the tribunal members can make a determination as to whether they have a conflict with a funder. The name of the funder and/or those who control it should be enough for purposes of conflict of interest.

ICSID is not the only or even the first institution to have adopted disclosure rules. For example, both the Singapore International Arbitration Centre (SIAC) and the Hong Kong International Arbitration Centre (HKIAC) adopted disclosure requirements for third-party funding in 2017 and 2018, respectively.

SIAC's disclosure requirements, which are potentially more expansive than ICSID's, apply only to arbitrations of investment disputes with

As third-party funding becomes increasingly mainstream and more frequently used, many arbitral institutions are seeking to amend their rules to include requirements pertaining to disclosure and notice.

states.[11] In other words, there is no explicit requirement under the SIAC Rules that parties in an international commercial arbitration must disclose any third-party funding arrangement. Conversely, Article 44 of the HKIAC Rules, which applies to all types of disputes, provides that:

> *if a funding agreement is made, the funded party shall communicate a written notice to all other parties [and] the arbitral tribunal ... of: (a) the fact that a funding agreement has been made; and (b) the identity of the third-party funder.*

In 2021, the International Chamber of Commerce (ICC) amended its rules to provide for disclosure of the existence of funding in a manner similar to ICSID and HKIAC. Rule 11(7) provides:

> *Each party must promptly inform the Secretariat, the arbitral tribunal and the other parties, of the existence and identity of any non-party which has entered into an arrangement for the funding of claims or defences and under which it has an economic interest in the outcome of the arbitration.*

And in its 2016 Note to Parties and Arbitral Tribunals on the Conduct of Arbitration, the ICC made clear in Section D that the purpose of the disclosure obligation embodied in Article 11(7) is "[t]o assist arbitrators and prospective arbitrators in complying with their duty of disclosure".

3.2 Rules including discretionary disclosure of third-party funding

In contrast to the foregoing institutions, some other leading institutions have (to date) refused to adopt a requirement for disclosure. For example, in 2019 the Arbitration Institute of the Stockholm Chamber of Commerce (SCC) adopted a policy encouraging the disclosure of the identity of "any third party with a significant interest in the outcome" of an SCC arbitration.[12] The rationale behind the SCC policy is the same as that behind the other institutions' rules – particularly those promulgated by ICSID and the ICC – and the 2014 IBA guidelines: that is, a desire to prevent any actual or perceived conflicts of interest between an arbitrator's role and their private interests.[13]

The American Arbitration Association, which administers international arbitrations through its International Centre for Dispute Resolution (ICDR), also contains a clear discretionary rule (see ICDR Article 14(7)).[14]

Finally, the 2020 Rules of the London Court of International Arbitration and the United Nations Commission on International Trade Law (UNCITRAL) Rules also do not require the disclosure of third-party funding. However, at least with respect to the UNCITRAL rules, this is likely to change soon, as Working Group III continues to grapple with issues regarding third-party funding and investor-state dispute settlement disputes, including potential conflicts of interest.[15] Working Group III has noted that even though the trend in regulation is to require disclosure only of the existence of funding and the identity of the funder, "the question of whether disclosure ... should also extend to the terms of the funding agreement remains controversial".[16] While it remains to be determined what the UNCITRAL Rules will contain, it is possible that they will resemble the ICSID and ICC rules to avoid inconsistent standards.

Notes

1 For example, the law of the jurisdiction in which the counsel for the parties practise or where each party resides, or the law of the seat of arbitration.
2 [2006] EWHC 839 (Comm).
3 [2017] EWHC 2805 (Ch).
4 [2018] EWHC 856 (Admin).
5 In a single case funding arrangement, a funder's connection to a claimant is based on a specific dispute because, ordinarily, the only assets to which a funder is entitled in exchange for its financing of the case are the case proceeds awarded in that specific dispute.
6 IBA Guidelines, Part I, General Standard (2)(b).
7 Rule 14(1) states: "A party shall file a written notice disclosing the name and address of any non-party from which the party, directly or indirectly, has received funds for the pursuit or defense of the proceeding ... in return for remuneration dependent on the outcome of the proceeding ('third-party funding'). If the non-party providing funding is a juridical person, the notice shall include the names of the persons and entities that own and control that juridical person."
8 Emphasis added. Rule 19(3)(b) reads: "[A]fter receipt of the request for acceptance of an appointment, the appointee shall ... provide a signed declaration ..., addressing matters including the arbitrator's independence, impartiality, availability and commitment to maintain the confidentiality of the proceeding."
9 Rule 14(4) states: "The Tribunal may order disclosure of further information regarding the funding agreement and the non-party providing funding pursuant to Rule 36(3)."
10 Unlike Rule 14, Rule 36(3) is a rule of evidence. It states that the "Tribunal may call upon a party to produce documents or other evidence if it deems it necessary at any stage of the proceeding".
11 Rule 24(l) of the 2017 SIAC Investment Rules, "Additional Powers of the Tribunal", reads: "Unless otherwise agreed by the Parties ..., the Tribunal shall have the power to ... order the disclosures of the existence of a Party's *third-party funding arrangement* and/or the identity of the third party-funder and, *where appropriate, details of the third party funder's interest in the outcome of the proceedings, and/or whether or not the third-party funder has committed to undertake adverse costs liability*" (emphasis added).
12 See SCC Policy on Disclosure of Third Parties with an Interest in the Outcome of the Dispute, 11 September 2019, https://sccarbitrationinstitute.se/sites/default/files/2022-11/scc-policy-re-third-party-interests-adopted.pdf.
13 The SCC's published policy document states that arbitrators should "take the information disclosed into account in making any disclosure or statement of independence and impartiality pursuant to Article 18 of the SCC Rules". Article 18 requires arbitrators to disclose "any circumstances that may give rise to justifiable doubts as to the arbitrator's impartiality or independence".
14 Under ICDR Article 14(7), the tribunal, either on its own initiative or upon the application of a party, may require the parties to disclose:

a. *Whether any non-party [including a third-party funder] has undertaken to pay or to contribute to the cost of a party's participation in the arbitration, and if so, to identify the person or entity concerned and to describe the nature of the undertaking.*
b. *Whether any non-party [including a third-party funder] has an economic interest in the outcome of the arbitration, and if so, to identify the person or entity concerned and to describe the nature of the interest.*

15 Particular situations include where arbitrators act as advisers to funders; and where an arbitrator or an arbitrator's law firm has a recurring relationship with a third-party funder which is involved in arbitration before the arbitrator and the arbitrator or the firm receives income from this relationship. A/CN.9/WG.III/WP. 157, para 18.
16 *Ibid*, paras 21–22. Further, in 2021, the UNCITRAL Secretariat published an initial draft of the provisions regulating third-party funding in investor-state dispute settlement. See Working Group III: Investor-State Dispute Settlement Reforms, https://uncitral.un.org/en/working_groups/3/investor-state and Initial Drafts on Reform Options, https://uncitral.un.org/en/draftworkingpapers. This draft

not only provides for the mandatory disclosure by the funded party to the tribunal and the other disputing party of the identity of the funder (and any controlling party in it), but also requires disclosure of the funding agreement or the terms thereof. In addition, the draft provides that the tribunal "may" require the funded party to disclose any of the following:

- whether the third-party funder agreed to cover the costs of an adverse cost award;
- the expected return amount of the third-party funder;
- any rights of the third-party funder to control or influence the management of the claim and to terminate the funding arrangement;
- the number of cases in which the third-party funder has provided funding for claims against the respondent state;
- any agreement between the third-party funder and the legal counsel or firm representing the funded party; and
- any other information deemed necessary by the tribunal.

See *ibid.*

VII. Costs and security for costs

Steven Friel
Woodsford

1. Introduction

1.1 Adverse costs

Many jurisdictions around the world – particularly those with an English common law tradition (eg, Australia and New Zealand) – apply a 'loser pays' principle to the costs of litigation. Also referred to as 'costs follow the event' or 'costs shifting', the principle empowers courts to order the losing party in litigation to pay a large proportion of the costs (legal fees and other disbursements) incurred by the winning party. These are often referred to as 'adverse costs'.

1.2 Security for costs

Where a defendant, during the course of litigation, has reasonable grounds to believe that the claimant bringing proceedings against it will ultimately be unable to meet an order for payment of adverse costs, it may apply to the court for an order that the claimant provide security for costs. Security may be provided in a number of ways – for example:

- a payment into a bank account held or supervised by the court;
- a payment into a trust account operated jointly by both the claimant's and defendant's solicitors; or
- provision of a contractual indemnity, possibly backed by insurance, directly to the defendant.

The security can be applied against any adverse costs order made against the claimant, with any balance returned to the claimant.

1.3 Litigation principles imported into arbitration

Many English litigation concepts – including, to some extent, costs rules – have been adopted into arbitration. This chapter looks at the adverse costs and security for costs position in both commercial arbitration and investor-state arbitration.

1.4 Relevance to third-party funding

The primary relevance of adverse costs and security for costs to third-party funding is perhaps obvious. The costs of arbitration are one of the major risks of arbitration and third-party funding offers a method of risk transfer. It may be that the third-party funder agrees to be liable for adverse costs and/or security for costs, or provides funding for an insurance premium to cover the risk. Further, English case law[1] and certain institutional rules provide that in certain circumstances, third-party funding costs are recoverable 'adverse costs', opening up the intriguing prospect of recalcitrant defendants being forced to pay the success fees owed by claimants to their litigation funders.

The primary relevance of adverse costs and security for costs to third-party funding is perhaps obvious. The costs of arbitration are one of the major risks of arbitration and third-party funding offers a method of risk transfer.

2. Adverse costs in arbitration: institutional rules

While arbitral panels generally have wide discretion in the allocation of costs, the principle of 'costs shifting' (ie, the loser pays the winner's costs) is prevalent in arbitration in numerous jurisdictions. Many arbitration rules expressly provide that the costs of arbitration shall in principle be borne by the unsuccessful party. For example, Article 28 of the 2020 Rules of Arbitration of the London Court of International Arbitration states:[2]

> *28.2 … The Arbitral Tribunal shall decide the proportions in which the parties shall bear such Arbitration Costs …*
>
> *28.3 The Arbitral Tribunal shall also have the power to decide by an order or award that all or part of the legal or other expenses incurred by a party (the 'Legal Costs') be paid by another party …*
>
> *28.4 The Arbitral Tribunal shall make its decisions on both Arbitration Costs and Legal Costs on the general principle that costs should reflect the parties' relative success and failure in the award or arbitration or under different issues, except where it appears to the Arbitral Tribunal that in the circumstances the application of such a general principle would be inappropriate under the Arbitration Agreement or otherwise. The Arbitral Tribunal may also take into account the conduct of the parties and that of their authorised representatives in the arbitration, including any cooperation in facilitating the proceedings as to time and cost and any noncooperation resulting in undue delay and unnecessary expense. Any decision on costs by the Arbitral Tribunal shall be made with reasons in the order or award containing such decision (unless it is a Consent Award).*

Other rules simply authorise the tribunal to make an award apportioning costs, without stating any presumption in favour of the 'costs follow the event' principle. For example, Article 38 of the 2021 Rules of Arbitration of the International Chamber of Commerce (ICC) states:[3]

> *4. The final award shall fix the costs of the arbitration and decide which of the parties shall bear them or in what proportion they shall be borne by the parties.*
>
> *5. In making decisions as to costs, the arbitral tribunal may take into account such circumstances as it considers relevant, including the extent to which each party has conducted the arbitration in an expeditious and cost-effective manner.*

Article 34 of the 2018 Arbitration Rules of the Hong Kong International Arbitration Centre states:[4]

> *34.1 The arbitral tribunal shall determine the costs of the arbitration in one or more orders or awards ...*
>
> *34.3 The arbitral tribunal may apportion all or part of the costs of the arbitration referred to in Article 34.1 between the parties if it determines that apportionment is reasonable, taking into account the circumstances of the case.*
>
> *34.4 The arbitral tribunal may take into account any third-party funding arrangement in determining all or part of the costs of the arbitration referred to in Article 34.1.*

Article 34.4 opens up the possibility that one party's costs of third-party funding – that is, the amount that that party is required to pay the third-party funder – could be recoverable from the other party. This is discussed in more detail in section 6 below.

3. Funder's liability for costs

A third-party funding agreement may provide that the funder will be liable for adverse costs and/or will obtain after-the-event insurance cover. It is not uncommon, for example, for third-party funders to indemnify the funded party in respect of adverse costs, usually limited by amount. It is also possible that a funding agreement will provide that if the funded party is ordered to make a payment for security for costs, that obligation will be met by the funder.

Aside from a contractual assumption of liability for adverse costs, do third-party funders have adverse costs risk? In court-based litigation in a number of jurisdictions, including England and Wales, the answer is clearly yes. However, in arbitration, the answer is probably no.

An English court's jurisdiction to deal with litigation costs is based on Section 51 of the Senior Courts Act 1981, which provides that the costs of civil litigation "shall be in the discretion of the court ... The court shall have full power to determine by whom and to what extent the costs are to be paid".[5]

It was once thought that Section 51 contained an implied limitation restricting its application to parties in the proceedings, and that the court could not order a non-party (eg, a litigation funder) to pay costs. However, in *Aiden Shipping v Interbulk*, Lord Goff stated:[6]

> *In the vast majority of cases, it would no doubt be unjust to make an award of costs against a person who is not a party to the relevant proceedings. But, as the facts of the present case show, that is not always so ... It is surely consistent with the interests of justice that, in such a case, the court's jurisdiction to make a global*

It is not uncommon, for example, for third-party funders to indemnify the funded party in respect of adverse costs, usually limited by amount.

> *order for costs relating to both sets of proceedings should not be fettered by the imposition of an implied limitation upon that Jurisdiction.*[7]

In a line of cases that includes *Arkin v Borchard Lines*,[8] *Excalibur Ventures LLC v Texas Keystone Inc*[9] and *Davey v Money*,[10] it has been established that the English courts' power to order third parties to pay adverse costs extends to litigation funders.[11]

While most arbitral tribunals have the power to order one of the parties to pay another party's costs, they do not have the power to order that a third party (a 'stranger' to the arbitration) – such as a litigation funder – pay adverse costs or security for costs. This is because arbitral tribunals have jurisdiction only over the parties which are bound by the arbitration agreement from which the arbitrators derive their power. Arbitral tribunals do not have an inherent jurisdiction in the same way that national courts do.

So, if third-party funders cannot be held liable for adverse costs or security for costs in arbitration, how might funding become relevant to the costs liabilities of the parties in arbitration? This question has arisen in two separate contexts: in litigation that follows arbitration and in investor-state arbitration.

4. Security for costs in litigation that follows on from arbitration
In *Progas Energy Limited v Pakistan*,[12] the claimants brought United Nations Commission on International Trade Law arbitration proceedings pursuant to the Mauritius-Pakistan Bilateral Investment Treaty. They were funded by Burford Capital. The tribunal rejected the claimants' claims and made an award of costs in Pakistan's favour. The claimants challenged the award under Section 68(2)(d) of the UK Arbitration Act 1996. Pakistan applied for security for:

- its costs in defending the challenge to the award; and
- the unpaid costs awarded to it by the tribunal.

The English High Court granted the former but rejected the latter.

As regards Pakistan's costs in defending the challenge to the award, the court considered the key questions to be:

- whether the claimants had sufficient assets; and
- whether those assets were available to meet any order for costs.

In correspondence, Burford had confirmed that it would satisfy an adverse costs order if the claimants failed to do so. However, the court found that Burford had made no legally enforceable commitment to either the claimants or Pakistan to meet an adverse costs order. Furthermore, in line with the decision of the underlying tribunal, the court rejected the claimants' argument that an order for security would be unfair since Pakistan's unlawful acts had caused the claimants' impecuniosity. The court ordered security of £400,000.

5. Security for costs in investor-state arbitration[13]
RSM Production Corporation v Saint Lucia[14] is an exceptional case. The claimant was supported by a third-party funder. The respondent relied on this fact when seeking an order of security for costs notwithstanding that the International Centre for Settlement of Investment Disputes (ICSID) Arbitration Rules in place at that time did not explicitly empower the tribunal to grant such an order[15] and no prior ICSID tribunal had ordered security for costs. However, the tribunal concluded from the claimant's conduct in other proceedings that there was a material risk that the claimant would not reimburse the respondent for its incurred costs. Further, the tribunal stated:

> *Moreover, the admitted third-party funding further supports the Tribunal's concern that Claimant will not comply with a costs award rendered against it, since, in the absence of security or guarantees being offered, it is doubtful whether the third-party will assume responsibility for honoring such an award. Against this background, the Tribunal regards it as unjustified to burden Respondent with*

the risk emanating from the uncertainty as to whether or not the unknown third-party will be willing to comply with a potential costs award in Respondent's favor.[16]

One of the arbitrators, Gavan Griffith QC, took the unusual step of providing additional assenting reasons for his support of the above finding. He stated that the business plan for a:

professional funder is to embrace the gambler's Nirvana: Heads I win, and Tails I do not lose ... [M]y position is that, unless there are particular reasons militating to the contrary, exceptional circumstances may be found to justify security of costs orders arising under BIT claims as against a third-party funder, related or unrelated, which does not proffer adequate security for adverse cost orders ... My determinative proposition is that once it appears that there is third-party funding of an investor's claims, the onus is cast on the claimant to disclose all relevant factors and to make a case why security for costs orders should not be made.[17]

Another arbitrator, Judge Edward Nottingham, issued a dissenting opinion:

19. The financing of ICSID arbitrations by persons or entities other than the parties themselves may well raise issues of general or particular concern. Should third-party funding ever be permitted? If so, under what conditions? Is such funding a legitimate tool allowing the pursuit of meritorious claims which otherwise could not be brought? Or is it a form of reprehensible barratry? What information about the nature of the funding or the identity of the funder should be relevant? What are the terms of the funding contract? Indeed, how is third-party funding defined? Would an insurance contract under which a State financed the defense of a case fit the definition?

20. There may be other issues raised by a regime concerning security for costs and the part which third-party funding may have in deciding whether and when security for costs may be appropriate. In my view, the general concerns about third-party funding and security for costs can and should be addressed by the Administrative Council in its rule-making capacity, if there is a problem that needs to be dealt with. Until the Administrative Council is more explicit about the matter, an individual tribunal should not be using general language of unlimited elasticity to accomplish the result which the tribunal regards as appropriate.[18]

In *EuroGas Inc and Belmont Resources Inc v Slovak Republic*,[19] the tribunal distinguished *RSM v Saint Lucia* as an outlier, in which:

> *an ICSID tribunal ordered security for costs. However, the underlying facts in that arbitration were rather exceptional since the claimant was not only impecunious and funded by a third-party, but also had a proven history of not complying with cost orders. As underlined by the arbitral tribunal, these circumstances were considered cumulatively.*[20]

The *EuroGas* tribunal concluded that:

> *no such exceptional circumstances have been evidenced in the instant case. The Claimants have not defaulted on their payment obligations in the present proceedings or in other arbitration proceedings. The Tribunal is of the view that financial difficulties and third-party funding – which has become a common practice – do not necessarily constitute per se exceptional circumstances justifying that the Respondent be granted an order of security for costs.*[21]

See also *South American Silver Limited v Bolivia*,[22] in which the tribunal started its analysis by noting that:

> *Security for costs (*cautio judicatum solvi*) is an instrument of English law that has been seen with certain reservations in arbitration in countries of other legal traditions. In investment arbitration, only in one case (*RSM v Saint Lucia*), the tribunal (with two strong separate and dissenting opinions) granted security for costs because it found circumstances that merited it.*

The tribunal continued:

> *the existence of a third-party that finances the claimant is not, by itself, a factor that should be taken into account in the determination of costs.*[23] *The Tribunal ... considers that it would not be consistent with such approach to consider the mere existence of a third-party funder as an exclusive factor to determine costs in an earlier stage of the proceedings, this is, in the evaluation of a request for security for costs.*
>
> *It is true that, as* Bolivia *affirms, one of the arbitrators in* RSM v Saint Lucia *suggested that the mere existence of a funder should be seen as a situation of exceptional circumstance and that the other party has the burden of proving the contrary, this is, to show that there is no exceptional case. However, the position of the majority was the opposite. Additionally, in the decision in* EuroGas v Slovak Republic, *cited by Bolivia, and which is subsequent to* RSM v Saint Lucia, *the tribunal stated that the mere existence of a third-party funder is not an exceptional situation justifying security for costs.*[24]

...

The Tribunal considers that while the existence of a third-party funder may be an element to be taken into consideration in deciding on a measure as the one requested by Bolivia, this element alone may not lead to the adoption of the measure.

The existence of the third-party funder alone does not evidence the impossibility of payment or insolvency. It is possible to obtain financing for other reasons. The fact of having financing alone does not imply risk of non-payment.

If the existence of these third parties alone, without considering other factors, becomes determinative on granting or rejecting a request for security for costs, respondents could request and obtain the security on a systematic basis, increasing the risk of blocking potentially legitimate claims.[25]

...

Finally, concerning the disclosure of the terms of the financing agreement entered into with the third-party funder, the Tribunal will reject such request.

Firstly, because, for the above-mentioned reasons, exceptional circumstances required to order security for costs are not present and the mere existence of the funder is not sufficient to order it. Therefore, it is not relevant under these particular circumstances to determine whether the third-party funder would assume or not an eventual costs award in favour of Bolivia.

Secondly, because no additional circumstances have been proven that, in the opinion of the Tribunal, warrant the modification of the decisions already taken concerning document production in the corresponding procedural phase.[26]

There was a different outcome in *García Armas v Venezuela*,[27] where the tribunal found that the claimants' reliance on third-party funding indicated a lack of funds and an increased risk of inability to pay costs – a risk exacerbated by the fact that the funding agreement did not cover adverse costs. The tribunal therefore decided that the claimants should bear the burden of demonstrating their ability to pay adverse costs. As the claimants failed to discharge this burden, the tribunal ordered security for costs.[28]

6. One party's liability for another party's funding costs

Commercial arbitrations are usually bound by strict confidentiality. There are therefore very few reported cases about third-party funding in commercial arbitration. One exceptional example is *Essar Oilfield Services Ltd v Norscot Rig Management Pvt Ltd*.[29]

In ICC arbitration, seated in London, before sole arbitrator Sir Philip Otton, well-resourced multinational Essar Oilfields Services Limited was held liable to pay damages to the much smaller Norscot Rig Management Pvt Limited for repudiatory breach of an operations management agreement. Essar was found liable to Norscot for the total sum of around $12 million, including around $4 million in respect of costs.

The arbitrator was highly critical of Essar's conduct towards Norscot, both during the currency of the agreement and for most of the arbitration period. The arbitrator found that Essar's conduct was so bad as to justify an order for indemnity costs – that is, at an enhanced rate.

The arbitrator held, among other things, that Norscot was entitled to the costs of litigation funding which it had obtained in order to bring the arbitration. The litigation funder, Woodsford, had provided £647,000 in funding and was entitled, in the event of Norscot's success, to a success fee. Norscot sought to recover that fee from Essar.

The arbitrator held that he was entitled so to order in his discretion, relying on both Sections 59 and 61 of the UK Arbitration Act 1996 and Article 31(1) of the 2012 ICC Rules (now contained in Article 38(1) of the 2021 rules).

The arbitrator said that "Essar had set out to cripple Norscot financially ... it was a David and Goliath battle".[30] He found that Norscot had no alternative but to enter into the litigation funding. Further, Norscot's funding costs reflected standard market rates.

The arbitrator observed that:

> *The magnitude of the arbitration resulted in a substantial amount for the claimant's costs in the region of US$3 million. Essar was undoubtedly aware that Norscot's costs could not be financed from its own resources ... and it was forced into 'litigation funding' ... It was blindingly obvious to [Essar] that the claimant was at a distinct financial disadvantage ... and would find it difficult if not impossible to pursue its claims by relying on its own resources. The respondent probably hoped that this financial imbalance would force the claimant to abandon its claims.*[31]

Essar challenged the costs order in proceedings before Judge Waksman QC in the English High Court, which had supervisory jurisdiction over the London-seated arbitration.

The judge referred to the *ICC Commission Report of 2015 on Decisions on Costs in International Arbitration*[32] and upheld the decision of the arbitrator.

While considered relatively controversial at the time, the decision in *Essar v Norscot* has since been endorsed by subsequent case law and by arbitral institutions.

In addition to Rule 34.4 of the 2018 Hong Kong International Arbitration Centre Arbitration Rules referred to in section 2 above, the 2021 Rules of the Australian Centre for International Commercial Arbitration refer to 'third-party funding costs' within the definition of 'the parties' legal and other costs', which are potentially recoverable by one party from another.

In *Tenke Fungurume Mining SA v Katanga Contracting Services SAS*,[33] the claimant in a London-seated ICC arbitration had received a third-party funding loan from an affiliate company and sought to recover this funding cost from the defendant. The defendant sought to attack that as an attempt to make an unwarranted return for the claimant's shareholder under the guise of costs recovery. The tribunal did not regard the fact that it was an intra-group loan as preventing recovery of the third-party funding fees – the important question instead being whether it had been reasonable under the circumstances for the claimant to resort to that loan as its means of funding. The defendant challenged the tribunal's decision under Section 68 of the 1996 act. The English High Court upheld the tribunal's decision, repeating the reasoning in *Essar v Norscot*.[34]

The author is grateful to colleague Karen Espinoza for her research and assistance in preparing this chapter.

Notes

1 *Essar Oilfield Services Ltd v Norscot Rig Management Pvt Ltd* [2016] EWHC 2361 (Comm).
2 www.lcia.org/Dispute_Resolution_Services/lcia-arbitration-rules-2020.aspx.
3 www.iccwbo.org/dispute-resolution-services/arbitration/rules-of-arbitration/.
4 www.hkiac.org/arbitration/rules-practice-notes/hkiac-administered-2018.
5 See also Rule 44.2 of the Civil Procedure Rules.
6 *Aiden Shipping Co Ltd v Interbulk Ltd* [1986] 2 WLR 1051.
7 *Aiden Shipping Co Ltd v Interbulk Ltd* [1986] AC 965, 980.
8 *Arkin v Borchard Lines Ltd* [2005] 1 WLR 3055.
9 *Excalibur Ventures LLC v Texas Keystone Inc* [2016] EWCA Civ 1144.
10 *Davey v Money* [2019] EWHC 997 (Ch).
11 There is a similar position in Australia. See, for example, *Wigmans v AMP Ltd (No 3)* [2019] NSWSC 162.
12 *Progas Energy Limited v Pakistan* [2018] EWHC 209 (Comm).
13 For a comprehensive analysis, see Xuan Shao, "Disrupt the gambler's nirvana: security for costs in investment arbitration supported by third-party funding", *Journal of International Dispute Settlement*, Volume 12, Issue 3, September 2021, pp427–447.

14 *RSM Production Corporation v Saint Lucia*, ICSID Case ARB/12/10. See also *Ioannis Kardassopoulos v The Republic of Georgia,* ICSID Case ARB/05/18 and ARB/07/15, Award, 3 March 2010.
15 The position is now explicitly governed by Rule 53 of the ICSID Arbitration Rules. See www.icsid.worldbank.org/sites/default/files/Arbitration_Rules.pdf.
16 *RSM Production Corporation v Saint Lucia*, ICSID Case ARB/12/10, Decision on Saint Lucia's Request for Security for Costs, 13 August 2014, para 83.
17 *Ibid*, paras 13, 16 and 18.
18 *Ibid*, dissenting opinion of Edward Nottingham, paras 19–20.
19 *EuroGas Inc v Slovak Republic,* ICSID Case ARB/14/14.
20 *EuroGas Inc v Slovak Republic,* ICSID Case ARB/14/14, Procedural Order 3, Decision on Requests for Provisional Measures, 23 June 2015, para 122. See also *RSM Production Corporation v Saint Lucia*, ICSID Case ARB/12/10, Decision on the Respondent's Request for Security for Costs, 13 August 2014, para 86.
21 *EuroGas Inc v Slovak Republic,* ICSID Case ARB/14/14, Procedural Order 3, Decision on Requests for Provisional Measures, 23 June 2015, para 123.
22 *South American Silver Limited v Bolivia*, PCA Case 2013-15, Procedural Order 10, 11 January 2016, para 45. See also *Bay View Group LLC v Republic of Rwanda,* ICSID Case ARB/18/21, Procedural Order 6, 28 September 2020; *Dirk Herzig as Insolvency Administrator over the Assets of Unionmatex Industrieanlagen GmbH v Turkmenistan*, ICSID Case ARB/18/35, Decision, 27 January 2020; *Hope Services LLC v Republic of Cameroon*, ICSID Case Arb/20/2, Procedural Order 4, 21 May 2021; *Orlandini v Bolivia*, PCA Case 2018-39, Decision, 9 July 2019; *Tennant Energy LLC v Canada*, PCA Case 2018-54, Procedural Order 4, 27 February 2020.
23 *Ioannis Kardassopoulos v Republic of Georgia,* ICSID Cases ARB/05/18 and ARB/07/15, Award, 3 March 2010, para 691; *RSM Production Corp v Grenada,* ICSID ARB/05/14, Annulment Proceeding, Order of the Committee Discontinuing the Proceeding and Decision on Costs, 28 April 2011, pp18–19, para 68.
24 *South American Silver Limited v Bolivia,* PCA Case 2013-15, Procedural Order 10, 11 January 2016, paras 73–74. See also *EuroGas Inc v Slovak Republic*, ICSID Case ARB/14/14, Procedural Order 3, Decision on Requests for Provisional Measures, 23 June 2015, para 123.
25 *South American Silver Limited v Bolivia,* PCA Case 2013-15, Procedural Order 10, 11 January 2016, paras 75–77. See also *Gustav FW Hamester GmbH & Co KG v Ghana,* ICSID Case ARB/07/24, Award, 18 June 2010, para 15.
26 *South American Silver Limited v Bolivia*, PCA Case 2013-15, Procedural Order 10, 11 January 2016, paras 80–82.
27 *Manuel García Armas v Bolivarian Republic of Venezuela*, PCA Case 2016-08, Procedural Order 9, 20 June 2018.
28 See also *Eugene Kazmin v Republic of Latvia,* ICSID Case ARB/17/5, Procedural Order 6, 13 April 2020.
29 *Essar Oilfield Services Ltd v Norscot Rig Management Pvt Ltd*, [2016] EWHC 2361 (Comm).
30 *Ibid*, para 21.
31 *Ibid*, para 23.
32 https://iccwbo.org/publication/decisions-on-costs-in-international-arbitration-icc-arbitration-and-adr-commission-report/.
33 *Tenke Fungurume Mining S.A. v Katanga Contracting Services SAS* [2021] EWHC 3301 (Comm).
34 And also the approach of the House of Lords in *Lesotho Highlands Development Authority v Impregilo SpA* [2005] UKHL 43.

VIII. The role of funders during arbitration proceedings

Hasan Tahsin Azizagaoglu
Ayse Yazir
Bench Walk Advisors
Nishant Nath Singh
Stewarts

1. Introduction

The objective of this chapter is to highlight the distinct role of litigation funders in the arbitration process, describing the various levels of involvement by these entities. It emphasises how their financial expertise and risk assessment capabilities can offer support at different stages of the dispute. The role of litigation funders in the arbitration space has become increasingly significant, adding a layer of financial support and strategic guidance to parties engaged in disputes. Unlike traditional legal services providers, litigation funders primarily operate within the domain of financial services, offering capital to cover legal costs associated with arbitration proceedings in exchange for a share of the potential settlement or award. Their involvement spans various stages – from the genesis of the claim through execution of the litigation funding agreement (LFA) all the way to the conclusion of the proceedings – with each stage reflecting differing degrees of engagement. At the outset, funders may assist in assessing the viability of a case, evaluating its merits, potential legal and financial risks. Throughout the proceedings, they may provide ongoing financial support, enabling parties to navigate the complexities of arbitration without the financial burden. Moreover, funders often play a pivotal role in settlement discussions, leveraging their financial expertise to help the client secure a favourable outcome.

Within this spectrum of involvement, funders can range from 'hands-on' funders which actively participate in case strategy and management to more 'hands-off' funders which provide capital with minimal interference in legal matters. This dynamic interplay between legal and financial expertise underlines the evolving landscape of litigation funding in arbitration, in which collaboration between different stakeholders in a dispute and funders can optimise outcomes. Especially the funder's ability to structure financing arrangements efficiently for both clients and lawyers, and to assist the parties in achieving the best outcome in a dispute or finding the optimal strategy to maximise results in settlement discussions, is what renders its contribution valuable. Ultimately, the difference between a good case and a good funding opportunity is the pot of gold at the end of the rainbow.

2. Legal services providers versus financial services providers

It is important to differentiate between:

- litigation funders that operate as legal services providers; and
- those functioning as financial services providers.

The inherent reason behind this distinction arises from the fact that while litigation funders may appear to operate on similar principles,

While some lawyers may prefer oversight, experienced legal practitioners may find excessive legal scrutiny to be burdensome and a drag on the process. A funder with a hands-off approach might be more suitable for legal practitioners who prefer autonomy in managing the dispute.

the way they are structured or operate can vary significantly. While some funders attempt to handle all processes in-house, others may prefer to outsource certain tasks by collaborating with experts. It all boils down to the general ethos of the funder. Hence, while some function like legal services providers, others operate like financial services providers.

It is therefore common for litigation funders to have a team of ex-litigators or arbitration practitioners working alongside the legal team, reviewing submissions, discussing legal strategy and involving themselves closely in legal decisions. These funders take a hands-on approach throughout the arbitration proceedings. On the other hand, funders that adopt a financial services model are likely to take a more hands-off approach. They act more like bankers, supporting skilled lawyers and allowing them to lead the process. Therefore, understanding the level of involvement and the operational style of a litigation funder is extremely important when selecting one. While some lawyers may prefer oversight, experienced legal practitioners may find excessive legal scrutiny to be burdensome and a drag on the process. A funder with a hands-off approach might be more suitable for legal practitioners who prefer autonomy in managing the dispute.

3. Contemplating funding prior to or at the start of the proceedings

The biggest added value of a funder at the beginning of a dispute is a comprehensive analysis of the case from the outset. It will employ a robust method for analysing both legal and financial risks. Litigation funders typically base their assessment of potential cases on five key variables:

- damages;
- enforcement and recoverability;
- merits;
- the parties involved; and
- the legal team.

While the order of importance may vary among funders, these variables remain consistent. Depending on the model adopted by the funder, the way in which it assesses the case or handles the process will differ. For example, a funder that handles everything in-house may review this checklist with in-house experts and make a decision to provide funding (or not). On the other hand, a funder that has adopted a hands-off approach is likely to have a smaller team and, for example, may not have an in-house asset tracer. Consequently, it may wish to engage an asset tracer, a quantum expert and a legal expert in a specific area of law to make a well-informed decision.

This will affect the decision-making process of the funder and, consequently, the timeline. The process is likely to be longer with a traditional funder trying to handle everything in-house, as this involves different departments within the funder. Hence, a decision will take longer than with a funder that has a smaller team and outsources all the processes. Such a funder is likely to expedite things more efficiently than a funder that tries to handle everything in-house. Since there are fewer layers of approval and departments to navigate, clients can expect a smoother experience and a faster decision-making process.

The early-stage involvement of the litigation funder provides the initial stress test for the case, which is also beneficial for the legal team and the client, as the additional scrutiny facilitates a more comprehensive review of the case from the outset. In some cases, even if the funder decides not to invest in the opportunity, it may, in addition to sharing feedback on its decision, provide the client with all reports prepared by its experts. Additionally, when reviewing the case, the funder will be presented with the budget, including the costs of lawyers, experts and various other disbursements; this presents a unique opportunity for the client to receive detailed feedback on the budget.

4. During the course of the proceedings

Assuming that the initial stages yield a positive result and the parties end up signing an LFA, the funder will have certain requirements from the lawyers to ensure that it receives a sufficient update on the case and the budget. As previously mentioned, the extent of these reporting duties varies substantially between funders. The contribution of funders that act as legal services providers extends beyond financial means. They provide legal support to the client to bring the case to the finish line. They have experienced lawyers on their teams who are likely to have few years of practice under their belts, so they may provide feedback on each submission to the tribunal or go over each draft to shape the legal structure.

On the other hand, hands-off funders recognise that their greatest value to a dispute lies in their financial capabilities. These funders primarily act as financial specialists, prioritising risk assessment and structuring financing to support legal proceedings. Their expertise lies in pricing risk and creating efficient funding arrangements, enabling lawyers to concentrate on the case without worrying about cash flow. They ensure that the deal is structured in a cost-efficient manner and that, while lawyers stay within their budget, their payments are processed smoothly.

Funders have various methods to ensure that lawyers adhere to the budget initially provided to them. Funders' financial risk assessment

Funders have various methods to ensure that lawyers adhere to the budget initially provided to them. Funders' financial risk assessment relies heavily on the ratio between damages and the budget; an opportunity must be economically viable to pursue. The magic number is also known as the 1:10 ratio.

relies heavily on the ratio between damages and the budget; an opportunity must be economically viable to pursue. The magic number is also known as the 1:10 ratio. Otherwise, if the numbers are too tight – meaning that the budget is too high and the damages too low – the client might end up with a smaller portion of the award or settlement proceeds. Contrary to general perceptions, funders do not seek to receive the majority of the proceeds. Therefore, they might employ their own methods to monitor the lawyers' budget.

This is particularly helpful for the lawyers, as they may not be fully aware of their total spending. Budget tracking systems typically indicate how much is required at each stage of the case, with specific amounts allocated accordingly. Consequently, when the law firm submits its invoices over an agreed period – usually monthly – the funder can review the numbers. This system benefits the client by ensuring that the funder not only provides the necessary funds for the entire arbitration process but also ensures its cost effectiveness. Additionally, this method guarantees cash flow for the lawyers. Funders typically allow lawyers to reallocate funds across the different stages of the proceedings or to provide additional funding if needed (subject, of course, to the terms of the LFA). Some funders even include a contingency in the budget for emergencies. This financial exercise also offers valuable guidance when making decisions on experts. Funders have extensive experience with expert costs and can ensure that lawyers receive the best work at the right prices. This gives the legal team confidence in engaging with top experts, knowing that the funder will provide financial support to cover these costs.

5. Conclusion of the proceedings

Litigation funders possess extensive financial modelling knowledge combined with legal understanding, making them invaluable at assisting clients and lawyers with the evaluation of settlement options. While some funders may actively participate in negotiations, leveraging their expertise to achieve favourable outcomes, others limit their involvement to providing mathematical analyses to guide decision making. It is important for funders to refrain from overstepping boundaries and allow legal teams to lead negotiations while providing support as needed.

Therefore, the funder can still be involved in the final stages of arbitration proceedings in different ways. Beginning with settlement discussions, hands-on funders may attempt to steer the discussion to protect their interests. On the other hand, the real value of a funder in settlement discussions lies in providing the legal team and the client with financial guidance to understand their current circumstances and what an ideal settlement might look like. Ultimately, there will be costs incurred by the parties and, therefore, a certain amount of money will be deployed by the funder from the committed amount. This means that the returns of each party should be calculated properly to determine the ideal settlement area for the client, ensuring that once the funder and the lawyers have been paid, it will be left with a substantial amount that meets its expectations. Hence, this mathematical exercise should be the most important contribution of the funder during settlement discussions.

After an award has been given, funders can be involved in three different ways. First, the client may choose to sell the claim and monetise it rather than waiting for enforcement. In this scenario, the funder pays an upfront payment and takes the risk of enforcement. Second, the funder may cover the costs of the enforcement process. Some funders have in-house enforcement specialists who oversee the entire process; while others prefer to engage with external asset tracers or enforcement specialists, depending on the types of assets or jurisdiction involved. In this capacity, as financial services providers, they fund the lawyers to engage with the best asset tracers and allow the lawyers to run the process. The third and final alternative is a hybrid model whereby the funder makes an initial upfront payment and then provides funding for enforcement. Once enforcement is successful, it makes a back-end payment.

In summary, litigation funders play a unique and valuable role in the arbitration process, providing financial support and strategic guidance to the parties involved in disputes. By leveraging their legal understanding and their expertise in risk assessment and financial modelling, funders contribute to the efficient management of cases in pursuit of favourable outcomes for clients. However, it is essential for funders to operate within regulatory and ethical frameworks, ensuring transparency and respecting the autonomy of legal teams and clients throughout the arbitration process.

IX. Funding and enforcement

Craig Arnott
Michael Redman
Mick Smith
Burford Capital

1. Introduction

Companies often spend years and considerable amounts of money on pursuing claims in international arbitration disputes, only to find that winning a claim and obtaining an arbitral award is just the first step in the process. Enforcement and recovery of the award require still more time and money. Further, arbitration awards may be subject to set-aside risk and the additional costs of those proceedings. Thus, at the end of an arbitration process, claimants can be left with an award on paper but no immediate or easy prospect of recovery.

The most common approach after winning a claim is for the award creditor to commence recognition and enforcement in jurisdictions where the award debtor has (or is likely to have) assets. However, this is not always a straightforward process. The recognition of an award by a national court is a prerequisite for the enforcement of any award and is usually treated under the New York Convention or relevant domestic legislation. Depending on the national court in question, this can itself be a protracted process.

Then, when the losing side in a dispute refuses to pay or hides assets in secretive jurisdictions, companies can face a potentially long and expensive road to enforcement and eventual recovery of the damages they are owed. This is, of course, in addition to the financial damages incurred as a result of the rule-breaking behaviour that was the subject of the original dispute. The successful party will also have incurred significant legal fees and expenses throughout the arbitration.

Companies, by their nature, are rarely designed to pursue costly and time-consuming litigation and enforcement proceedings. On average, commercial claims in England and Wales take around 15 to 18 months just to get to trial,[1] with the average London Court of International Arbitration proceeding lasting around 16 months to resolve plus an additional three months to produce awards (large commercial cases with over $100 million in dispute last on average 29 months). Investor-state matters take even longer: International Centre for Settlement of Investment Disputes matters take 3.86 years to resolution plus an additional 13.3 months between the close of a final hearing and the issuance of an award.[2]

Since a company's financial circumstances might change drastically in the years waiting for matters to resolve, businesses need to consider the impact of having working capital out the door for a potentially lengthy period of time. This may lead claimants to consider outside financing for their matters. Again, duration is an equally important consideration for companies considering their options as to legal

Since a company's financial circumstances might change drastically in the years waiting for matters to resolve, businesses need to consider the impact of having working capital out the door for a potentially lengthy period of time.

finance partners. Privately held legal finance companies have funds which have a finite period of time in which to invest the capital committed to them: they need to return capital to investors and terminate the fund after a certain period. In contrast, a publicly listed legal finance company functions as a conventional operating business with perpetual life and its own balance sheet. Capital belongs to the legal financier permanently; it does not need to be returned to investors.

Given the typical length of the initial arbitration, companies frequently experience dispute fatigue and can be reluctant to enforce awards that seem to involve drawn-out battles with recalcitrant award debtors. The immediate cost of enforcing an award may carry more weight in commercial analysis than the possibility of recovering some money later. Macro-economic trends such as recessions or market turbulence may also encourage companies to spend their working capital to support business operations rather than hiring lawyers to enforce an award after an already expensive and protracted arbitration process.

As a result, many companies can have valuable unenforced judgments, arbitral awards and uncollected recoveries. In a 2020 study, 70% of in-house lawyers reported that their companies had unenforced judgments valued at $20 million or more.[3]

In this chapter, we address some of the key issues with enforcement in the arbitration context and explore how funded asset recovery or award assignment can help claimants to recover what they are owed.

2. Issues for award enforcement in commercial arbitration

In the commercial arbitration context, the most common challenges in award enforcement are finding and seizing assets.

Award debtors can employ many tactics that pose obstacles to enforcement. The award debtor could be a special purpose company with no assets of its own. Award debtors can reside in or move to a jurisdiction where enforcement and asset tracing are more difficult. The divergent approaches taken in different jurisdictions can prove difficult to navigate when enforcing awards. For example, many jurisdictions lack publicly available corporate information, particularly regarding shareholders and ultimate beneficial owners of companies. Even where disclosure of ownership information is required, many companies fail to comply, use nominees or otherwise provide false or misleading information.

Even in the United States, which typically has broad discovery rules under a Section 1782 application, the recent US Supreme Court decision in *ZF Automotive* limits the availability of Section 1782 discovery in certain commercial arbitrations. In this unanimous decision, the court held that:

- a 'foreign or international tribunal' is one that exercises governmental authority; and
- neither private commercial arbitration panels nor *ad hoc* arbitration panels assembled under international treaties – even with a sovereign as a party – qualify under Section 1782.

This ruling will make the finding of assets to satisfy awards harder in the United States.[4]

If the debtor doesn't want to pay, numerous common tactics can frustrate recovery. Debtors often hide assets in complex corporate structures and claim impecuniousness when enforcement is attempted. As one example of a poverty plea, an individual debtor could claim to be a beneficiary of a discretionary trust in which the debtor has no entitlement to trust assets. Pursuing those assets requires proving that the trust is a sham, which often entails an expensive and time-consuming fight, likely crossing several jurisdictions.

Bad debtors will use any opportunity to draw out an enforcement process with the aim of racking up pursuit costs and delaying collection until the award creditors eventually give up or run out of money. For example, they might initiate set-aside proceedings or make unfounded allegations of bias and corruption with the arbitral process.

Another tactic commonly employed is for debtors to reduce the value and equity of an identified enforceable asset by leveraging against it. Debtors may claim that they can no longer afford their legal teams and need to secure legal expenses against the asset in question – effectively cannibalising the asset so that it is no longer available for collection. Alternatively, a debtor may disperse enforceable assets to third parties – commonly family members – by transferring assets for zero or nominal consideration around the same time that it learns it is vulnerable to enforcement proceedings.

For these reasons, it is best to engage asset recovery experts at the outset, when the arbitral award is issued, to help with an effective recovery strategy.

3. Issues for award enforcement in investor-state arbitration

The enforcement of arbitration awards is often even more challenging when claimants are pursuing payment from a sovereign state, which will often have immunity protections or use complex ownership

Bad debtors will use any opportunity to draw out an enforcement process with the aim of racking up pursuit costs and delaying collection until the award creditors eventually give up or run out of money.

structures of state-sponsored bodies that present obstacles to enforcement.

Sovereign immunity is a legal doctrine that grants sovereigns and states immunity from civil suits or criminal prosecution and represents the greatest challenge for claimants in their enforcement efforts against sovereign debtors. Sovereign immunity can be invoked to assert that tribunals and courts do not have jurisdiction over states, thus potentially preventing the enforcement of an award against state assets at home or abroad. In some jurisdictions, sovereign immunity is absolute, while in others it is more qualified.

However, the primary immunity issue is generally waived in the context of a treaty arbitration award. Then, the enforcement issues are generally:

- whether the asset in question is owned by the state or a state-owned entity non-debtor; and
- whether the asset is being used for commercial or sovereign purposes.

As a result, the burden falls to claimants to distinguish between the acts of a sovereign and those of a purely commercial nature. This hurdle, known as the commercial purpose test, requires parties seeking enforcement against a sovereign state to establish that relevant assets are purely commercial in nature or intent.[5]

The volume and variety of assets owned by a sovereign and a sovereign state's inherent lack of transparency could create additional challenges to enforcement. States may use complex ownership structures, restructuring and ostensible privatisation as a tactical manoeuvre to obscure, dissipate or otherwise firewall assets, enabling them to claim that they lack the requisite levels of control over money-making interests. It is also common for states to use set-aside proceedings as a delay tactic: states are usually granted a stay on enforcement for a period of two years or longer while set-aside or annulment proceedings are pending.

States must pay their debts, including adverse arbitral awards, with taxpayer funds. Therefore, efforts to avoid or delay payment may be met with support by constituents and may at times be justified in nationalistic or ideological terms. Too often, enforcement efforts can be influenced by politics, which could be more easily avoided by a well-considered enforcement strategy. Further, in the event of a sovereign's inability to pay an award, there are no rules and no centralised authority governing sovereign bankruptcy.

Too often, enforcement efforts can be influenced by politics, which could be more easily avoided by a well-considered enforcement strategy.

In either case, claimants face the risk of being unable to recover on their award. And as states become increasingly comfortable with what may be (or is perceived to be) the limited consequences of non-payment, these challenges have become even more pronounced.

4. Asset recovery and funded award enforcement

Asset recovery expertise helps clients to overcome the factual and legal hurdles that stand in the way of recovering money where a favourable award has been rendered but the opponent hides assets or fails to pay. Essentially, asset recovery delivers actionable intelligence and transforms award debt from 'legal paper' into cash.

Legal finance can be used in the enforcement context to remove the common imbalance that claimants face compared to award debtors and shift the cost and risk of recovering assets to satisfy the award (which can too often cause claimants to feel it is easier to walk away, resulting in unrealised assets worth tens of millions) to a third party.

Given the sometimes substantial and unanticipated cost of recovery once an award is obtained – not to mention the risk inherent in any enforcement procedure – asset recovery finance is becoming an increasingly popular tool for law firms and companies.

A client seeking assistance in enforcing an award can engage a legal finance provider to provide financing to pay the costs of enforcement and any ongoing set-aside proceedings in exchange for a share of the recovery. The legal financier provides investigative input and case management across jurisdictions. The central benefit is that because the funding is provided on a non-recourse basis, the claimant need only repay the legal finance provider once a recovery has occurred and has no obligation should the award not be recovered. This protects the company from any downside risk in pursuing assets while simultaneously unlocking and preserving the potential for return in the event of a successful enforcement.

Asset recovery financing can take a variety of forms, including the following:

- The funder can provide asset recovery services on a full or partial contingency basis – that is, a client seeking assistance to enforce an award will engage a legal finance company to provide financing of an enforcement in exchange for a share of the recovery.
- The funder can provide advisory services for investigation of assets and recovery strategy during the arbitration phase or post-award.
- The funder can monetise the award by purchasing all or a

portion of the award and taking full responsibility for enforcing the award – a transaction that results in immediate liquidity to the claimant.

We have found that asset recovery can be most efficiently financed when the expertise of asset tracing resides under the same roof as legal finance, which can provide important synergies for claimants.

Worked example: multi-jurisdictional enforcement of an International Chamber of Commerce award[6]

Following a breach of contract dispute, global construction company ACME Ltd received an arbitral award from an International Chamber of Commerce tribunal for $80 million. The company then faced years of complex, high-cost multi-jurisdictional enforcement proceedings across many jurisdictions – including Dubai, Liechtenstein, The Bahamas and the United States – to unlock the latent value of the award.

The legal finance provider funded the enforcement of this award against the worldwide assets of the award debtor and provided $10 million upfront to ACME. The legal finance provider conducted investigative work and court proceedings in jurisdictions around the globe, while ACME de-risked its recovery effort and transformed its pending award into cash that it was able to reinvest into business operations. Following numerous successes over a three-year period, the matter settled successfully in favour of the client and the funder received its full contractual entitlement of $30 million and its investment back, with the client retaining $40 million of the final award without having to take on any enforcement risk.

5. Assignment of arbitral awards

Another option available to award creditors is to sell or 'assign' an award of damages to a third party. Because an arbitral award is an asset on the company's books, it can be compared to owning the benefit of a debt receivable. Therefore, companies are generally free to assign or transfer the award in the same way as they would other sorts of receivables.

The process of selling the award can take many forms. Typically, many award creditors reach out directly in order to engage asset recovery assistance and discuss options to monetise the award. At its most basic, 'monetisation' simply means a payment for an award from a third party, such as a legal finance company. Monetising an award can result in a 100% assignment of the award or create a scenario where the award creditor retains a benefit from the later financial enforcement of that award. Sometimes, to gauge the market's interest, an award creditor may use an auction process which is typically run by a broker or a financial intermediary such as a bank. In those circumstances, the seller usually prepares documents for potential purchasers, which can include basic information about the award, a non-disclosure agreement and access to data for due diligence. Following due diligence, prospective buyers of the award then provide a bid along with any terms for consideration.

Assigning an award relieves the claimant of the cost and time burden of enforcing it and generates upfront capital at the time of assignment without delay or having to incur further legal spend. Importantly, certain structures allow the award creditor to potentially retain a stake in the future recovery. The injection of capital from the assignment allows the claimant to invest directly into its business without exposure to the risk of challenges to awards, whether in the form of a reduction of damages or a reversal or set-aside of an award. Arbitral awards may be assigned to commercial legal finance providers in a number of different complex structures, depending on the circumstances of the case and the award creditor.

It has become common practice for legal finance providers to look at arbitral awards with a view to purchasing them. For claimants, award assignment has the additional advantage of relatively lower cost of capital than other forms of legal finance in which litigation risk

Sometimes, to gauge the market's interest, an award creditor may use an auction process which is typically run by a broker or a financial intermediary such as a bank.

remains. Given that the proceedings have settled and the award has been finalised subject to set-aside, the risk to the legal finance provider can be greatly reduced, resulting in generally more attractive terms for award creditors. In these instances, the parties may be able to offer on a lower return for the funder's capital than in conventional, binary single-case litigation finance arrangements.

Legal finance providers typically consider the following criteria when considering an award assignment:

- Award size: A legal finance provider will look for an award with substantial damages. This is typically to accommodate the fact that there is a discount applied from the face value of the award plus any ancillary costs that the funder must take on for enforcement, set-aside or annulment.
- Respondent profile: The more likely it is that the funder will be able to enforce the award against the respondent, the more likely the funder is to finance the enforcement. If the award is against a sovereign, the funder will consider its track record and timeline for paying awards. If the award debtor is a commercial entity, the funder will similarly consider what diligence and asset tracing work has revealed about its history of paying previous awards and its assets around the world.
- Counsel: Funders will also examine what counsel is in place to handle a set-aside or annulment, as well as enforcement.

Funders tailor award assignment agreements to suit client needs by adopting structures that meet client requirements and expectations. Every structure is bespoke to a particular transaction or award. For example, the award assignment could be in return for one lump-sum payment or multiple payments tied to trigger events in the future. The deal could follow a dual payment structure consisting of a payment on closing and then a payment on the conclusion of a set-aside proceeding; or even a tripartite structure with three payments – one on closing, one on inclusion of the set-aside and one on collection of proceeds.

Worked example: assignment of an award against a sovereign state[7]

Peerless Inc had an international award of $300 million against a sovereign state entity following a straightforward trade dispute. Problematically, by the conclusion of the lengthy arbitration proceedings, the particular trading entity had been wound down – so recourse lay against the state itself, which refused all attempts to pay. Peerless faced the prospect of embarking on a lengthy enforcement battle with the state or abandoning its claim and writing off its legal costs. The business wanted to invest in new technologies for competitive growth, so the finance department did not want to spend additional moneys pursuing payment for the award debt from the state.

Peerless decided to partially assign its award to an experienced legal finance provider for an immediate lump-sum payment of $25 million and retain some later participation in the award. The lump-sum payment provided immediate liquidity to Peerless that could be invested in highly profitable business opportunities during the enforcement of its $300 million award. The upfront liquidity did not create debt: Peerless knew that if the award was not successfully enforced, it would keep the $25 million and the benefit to its business – and owe the legal finance provider nothing.

Peerless repaid the legal finance provider its $25 million plus an agreed percentage of the award after it was paid following a two-year enforcement process, with Peerless retaining the remaining damages, net the funder's return. And because the company had access to $25 million of its recovery early – equivalent to $31 million after two years at the 12% annual rate of growth for its target opportunities – it was able to continue to grow its business (and its profits) while the award was undergoing enforcement.

6. Conclusion

Ultimately, obtaining an arbitration award is just the first step in a claimant getting the money it is owed. Although the road to enforcement can be difficult – particularly when dealing with states or sophisticated commercial parties – there are ways to de-risk and alleviate the costs of pursuing arbitral awards. Whether by funding an enforcement effort or by assigning an award partially or outright to a legal finance provider, companies can leverage risk-free capital to bolster cash and invest in their businesses, recovering substantial value for their hard-won arbitral awards without the litigation cost to their business of funding enforcement itself.

Notes

1 Maria Daniel, Michelle Radom and Salome Sanz, "Litigating across Europe – timing is everything", Lexology, 27 September 2022, www.lexology.com/library/detail.aspx?g=281d57ba-f665-41eb-b36c-c347f11e2ac1.

2 Jeffery Commission and Rahim Moloo, *Procedural Issues in International Investment Arbitration*, Oxford International Arbitration Series (OUP 2018), https://oxia.ouplaw.com/display/10.1093/law/9780198729037.001.0001/law-9780198729037#:~:text=Jeffery%20Commission%2C%20Rahim%20Moloo&text=The%20book%20takes%20the%20reader,details%20of%20the%20relevant%20precedents.

3 Burford Capital, *2020 Legal Finance Report*, 16 October 2020, www.burfordcapital.com/insights/insights-container/2020-legal-finance-report/.

4 *ZF Automotive US Inc v Luxshare Ltd*, No 21-401.

5 Phoebe Waters, "How an asset recovery team can help enforce against a sovereign state", *Global Arbitration Review*, 8 October 2020, https://globalarbitrationreview.com/article/how-asset-recovery-team-can-help-enforce-against-sovereign-state.

6 This example is illustrative and does not represent an actual funded matter.

7 This example is illustrative and does not represent an actual funded matter.

X. Avoiding and managing disputes with funders

Julian Chamberlayne
Stewarts

1. Introduction

If a client has a high-value dispute with attractive merits, economics and duration, it is likely that it will be able to secure litigation funding. However, the financial and other terms of litigation funding agreements can vary in several important ways concerning:

- the control of the litigation;
- the flexibility to respond to developments; and
- ultimately, the balance of the proceeds left for the client.

The termination provisions and priorities agreement for the order of the distribution of the proceeds are particularly important.

Consequently, it is sensible for parties seeking alternative funding agreements to choose their providers and negotiate terms carefully. Disputes between the client, instructed lawyers, funders and/or after-the-event (ATE) insurers can be a serious distraction from the underlying proceedings; hence, upfront measures to reduce the risk of funding-related disputes and provide for their swift and effective resolution if they arise are well worth exploring.

2. Identifying and selecting a suitable funder

An early step in securing funding is to identify one or more suitable funders. Because the pricing and terms of litigation funding agreements vary significantly, the choice of funder is crucial. While third-party funding has been available for several decades, the lawyers instructed by the claimant for their dispute may have limited recent experience of working with a variety of funders. If that is the case, they ought to consider whether it is in the client's best interests to instruct a funding broker or for a law firm that specialises in advising clients on alternative funding agreements to advise independently on those discrete issues.

A funded claimant may prefer independent advice if it wants to be represented in the negotiations for an alternative funding agreement (eg, a conditional fee agreement (CFA) or damages-based agreement) with the law firm it has instructed to conduct the substantive arbitration or litigation. Alternatively, some well-resourced corporate or institutional claimants may have general counsel who are sufficiently experienced in litigation funding to address this issue in-house, without external representation.

Whoever is advising the claimant on the funding issues should conduct due diligence to probe each prospective funder's capital adequacy and ability to meet any security for costs requirements. This due diligence will usually involve:

While third-party funding has been available for several decades, the lawyers instructed by the claimant for their dispute may have limited recent experience of working with a variety of funders.

- identifying funding entities and their owners/controllers;
- confirming the funder's own anti-money laundering and sanctions monitoring;
- establishing the size of relevant funds and the proportion of those funds already allocated;
- ring-fencing funds, including through compliance with the Association of Litigation Funders' requirements;
- establishing whether the funder has the ability to provide an indemnity for adverse costs either from its own funds or via its own insurance arrangements;
- identifying:
  - potential conflicts of interest with other funded cases/clients; and
  - the funder's ability to establish internal information barriers and its procedures to preserve confidentiality and privilege;
- identifying whether the funder has been subject to any prior court or arbitral orders in previous cases or disputes with clients;
- determining whether the funder has experience of the type of dispute in question; and
- requesting a reference from a well-regarded law firm or corporate that has recently worked with the funder, ideally through to a late stage in the proceedings.

The next point of advice from the law firm and decision for the client is whether to approach a single funder or approach more than one funder simultaneously, sometimes referred to as conducting a 'beauty parade'.

Some clients or the law firms they have instructed may have a strong pre-existing working relationship with a single funder. It is also possible that their choice may be constrained by a pre-existing portfolio funding agreement (the pros and cons of which are outside the scope of this chapter).

Preparing a compelling proposal and negotiating heads of terms with a single funder take time and command a decent budget. Clearly, that budget will be larger for a beauty parade than a single funder approach. However, if through that process the price of funding a substantial dispute can be secured for, say, 0.5x less through seeking and receiving competitive bids from a number of funders, that could result in a net improvement in the outcome of the dispute running into the millions. The value of improvements to other terms of funding beyond pricing should also not be underestimated.

The other notable advantage of pursuing discussions with multiple funders is that it de-risks the scenario of a single preferred funder declining the case at a late stage, causing delay and disruption to the plans for advancing the claim or even commencing proceedings.

Before approaching funder(s), one of the key issues to resolve is how much funding is required. Surprisingly, this seemingly simple proposition is often not given the attention it deserves, as getting it wrong can lead to significant problems later. The budget needs to be realistic at the outset to minimise the risk of having to go 'cap in hand' to the funder later to request an increase. All too often, the preliminary cost estimates are prepared on a top-down basis, with a view to either winning the client's instructions or keeping it happy (for now) by quoting a lower cost than is realistic, bearing in mind the many events that can and do arise during complex and high-value commercial or investor treaty disputes. Provided that you have established a good dialogue with the funder, it will tell you whether it thinks your budget or contingencies are higher than its investment committee would approve and give you the opportunity to reconsider how the budget is presented.

With the assistance of an experienced cost lawyer, a realistic budget with appropriate assumptions and contingencies should be carefully crafted. The budget should be prepared from the bottom up, carefully considering what work is required for each substantive task in each phase of the proceedings. Ideally, any external providers whose services will come at a significant cost should be asked to give preliminary quotes. The budget should also include provision for the likely cost of any ATE insurance premiums, including any additional cost for the insurers to provide an anti-avoidance endorsement or deed to satisfy any security for cost requirements.

However, if the budget is larger than can be borne by a realistic appraisal of the value of the likely claim proceeds, it can kill the proposition from the outset. So, having prepared the full 'bottom-up' cost estimate, it is time to consider its impact on the economic viability of the action. In some cases, that may involve difficult conversations around whether the law firm is prepared to put more of its fees at risk and/or for the client to fund aspects of the expenditure to reduce the funding requirement. It may even cause a change in litigation strategy to attempt to reduce the number of opposing parties or narrow the claim or issues within the dispute. While these may be awkward issues, they are better confronted at the outset than later, by which time it may be too late with the funding having run dry.

Equally important as a realistic budget is the accompanying funding proposal and related document pack that must be prepared and submitted to the funder(s). Most law firms are good at describing the legal issues and complexities. Many thrive on the intellectual challenge

Before approaching funder(s), one of the key issues to resolve is how much funding is required. Surprisingly, this seemingly simple proposition is often not given the attention it deserves, as getting it wrong can lead to significant problems later.

of thorny points of law. However, when preparing the summary of the claim in the funding proposal form, they should not lose sight of the broader issues that will influence the funder's decision. These include:

- the prospects that the case will settle;
- a realistic appraisal of the likely claims proceeds in a settlement;
- the likely time it will take to settle the claim;
- the distinct risks that could cause the claim to fail (as these are subject to the fourth law of probability);
- whether the client is likely to follow advice and make objectively commercial decisions at each stage; and
- the likelihood and timescale of any subsequent appeal or enforcement proceedings.

3. Negotiating heads of terms and the funding agreement

If the funder(s) are prepared to back the claim after conducting their due diligence, they usually set out their key terms in a heads of terms document. The claimant and any lawyers instructed to advise on funding will need to scrutinise these terms carefully and be prepared to negotiate on any that they seek to change.

With regard to pricing, the conventional options are for a percentage of the recoveries or a multiple of the amount funded, or the higher of both. Some funders propose pricing based on interest rates or to give them a certain level of internal rate of return. When it comes to multiples, it is important to consider whether that relates to the full funding commitment, tranches or just the funds drawn down. The amount of the funding premium will often be staged by duration, tranches of the amount committed or stages of the proceedings. Whatever pricing is proposed, it is important for anyone advising the claimant to model the likely impact of that funding in various realistic outcomes.

There is a long list of other important terms that should be considered at the heads of terms stage. Examples of some of the funding terms that can be suitable for some but not all cases include:

- staged funding on a multiple-only basis rather than a higher of multiple or percentage;
- break clause or low multiple to limit the funder's premium to a moderate monetary sum in early settlement scenarios;
- funder's premium on deployed (not committed) capital (or tranches);
- budget variation terms (eg, to reallocate phases) and the variation process to reduce the risk of later standoffs or uncertainty if unforeseen developments result in budget increases;
- funder's indemnity to provide for the risk of adverse costs exposure in excess of ATE insurance indemnities; and
- funder's indemnity for adverse costs, which avoids local insurance licensing issues and/or a high level of insurance premium tax if the claimant resides in a country with challenging insurance regulations.

Examples of the more problematic funding terms that some funders may try to incorporate in some cases include:

- immediate repayment of funding following the occurrence of a termination event, a decision that the funding is unlawful or a conflict of interest arising that prevents the funder from continuing to perform its obligations; and
- a term allowing the funder at any time to assign or transfer rights under the agreements at its sole discretion, potentially to another funder which may not have passed a rigorous due diligence assessment.

While negotiations concerning the priorities agreement (sometimes known as the 'waterfall') often only take place at the back end of negotiating all related alternative funding agreements, it is preferable to seek an outline agreement in the heads of terms. The advantages of this approach include the potential in some cases to:

- have a meaningful negotiation of the waterfall rather than being forced into accepting the funder's default priorities agreement;
- try to secure safeguards for the claimant in low recovery scenarios; and
- anticipate the involvement of additional stakeholders later and avoid the complication and uncertainty of negotiating subsequent changes to the waterfall.

Finally, in relation to heads of terms, the duration of any exclusivity period should be considered. This will need to balance:

- the funder's legitimate concern to avoid investing too much in a case that the claimant may never commit to incepting with it; and
- the claimant's concern to avoid being tied to one funder for too long prior to securing its investment committee's approval and finalising acceptable terms for the funding agreement.

The attention then turns to finalising a mutually acceptable funding agreement. These are complex, high-value contracts that warrant close attention. They will frequently require several rounds of negotiation, some of which may be best done face to face to try to cut through the issues. Any shortcuts or inattention to detail may come back to bite you or your client later.

4. Managing the relationship between claimant and funder

Having done the hard work of scrutinising and negotiating optimal terms for the funding agreement, you would be forgiven for thinking that things would be plain sailing from there on in. If only it were that simple. It remains important to manage the expectations of, and the relationship between, the claimant and funder throughout. Experience shows that managing relations between the claimant, funder and law firm can sometimes be as challenging and time-consuming as managing the substantive dispute.

Good communication is essential. At the outset of the case, you will need to establish a reporting framework in line with the terms of the funding agreement and any ATE insurance policy. Typically, this will involve providing monthly reports to the claimant, funder and insurance providers. This will ensure that all stakeholders are aware of any potential issues before (or at least as) they emerge, which makes them easier to manage. You will need to ensure that the claimant takes ownership of the issues, even though it is not directly paying for the legal work. It also needs to understand that open and fair communication with funders and insurers is essential to maintaining good relations and avoiding breaching duties, including providing ongoing full and frank disclosure.

It is advisable to involve an experienced costs lawyer as an integral member of the legal team from the outset. This will enhance the ability to provide accurate monthly reports and the reasoning behind any (potential) budget overages.

You will need to be alive to:

- the internal pressure that the funder is under (including its duties to its investors); and
- the funder's own internal budget limitations and restrictions.

The funder is often applying significant capital over a long period of time. It will thus exert a degree of control over the case, although the extent and expression of that control vary considerably from funder to funder. The obligations between each of the law firm, the funder and the claimant are different. The instructed lawyers should keep in mind that the funding agreement is between the funder and the claimant. At all stages, the lawyer's primary duty is to act in the client's best interests and to seek and follow its instructions. The lawyer should avoid treating the funder like a pseudo-client just because it is paying the bills.

It is advisable to involve an experienced costs lawyer as an integral member of the legal team from the outset. This will enhance the ability to provide accurate monthly reports and the reasoning behind any (potential) budget overages.

5. Managing the budget and dealing with budget variations/overage

Even with a carefully prepared and proactively monitored budget, countless issues can drive a case over budget during certain phases or overall. Often, no one in the claimant's camp will be to blame for this turn of events and all the stakeholders will need to work together to find ways to ensure the case does not stall or come to an end through lack of funding.

Claimants and their lawyers often need to turn to funders for a budget variation. If a clear process for such variations was agreed upon in the funding agreement, they will be on more solid ground. However, there may still be reasons why funders resist or stall a budget variation request. Examples include:

- exceeding the funder's internal damages to costs ratio (conventionally 10:1, although this can be lower with some funders in some cases);
- awaiting a development or stage in the case;
- exhausting a funding 'cell'; and
- becoming nervous about the case's merits (perhaps where a judgment in another case changes the funder's appetite to invest).

The consequent actions by a funder might be to request a report on assets or new strategies, a second opinion or even a change of counsel. When appropriate, it may be necessary to challenge such requests if the report/information has recently been provided or is inherently unlikely to make a real difference.

Be aware of where the fund is in its funding cycles, as this might dictate whether and how much uncommitted capital the funder has within that fund that is deployable to accommodate an increased budget. If necessary, ask probing questions to ascertain the position.

When budget overage is looming or has already been incurred, it is sometimes tempting for the instructed lawyer to try to agree a budget variation with the funder first and then present the client with an agreed package. However, that approach can catch the client by surprise and might strain relations between them and the law firm. The better first step is to secure the client's agreement to pursue a budget overage request with the funder on its behalf.

Virtually all funders appreciate that budget overages are common, but the terms of funding agreements commonly give funders wide-ranging discretion over whether to agree budget variations. Some funders go further by including clauses stating that any overages should be at the

Be prepared to discuss 'early' settlements with clients. An early settlement offer may appear to be less than what the client expects, but by settling on the steps of the court, proportionately more will be paid away to the funder.

law firm's full risk. Even when no such clauses exist, it is a common expectation of many funders. This scenario can create a mismatch in expectations between the client, law firm and funder that can be difficult to resolve.

If the decision on additional funding is delayed, substantial fees and disbursements can be run up with uncertainty over whether, when and by whom they will be paid. This uncertainty is unsettling for the client and the law firm. The need for a budget increase often comes at a later stage of a claim – potentially when there are crucial workstreams to complete and there is no easy option to halt work while funding issues are resolved. It is very uncomfortable to manage a situation where the law firm, external counsel and experts are working under time pressure and on an unanticipated and unagreed risk basis. That is why it is best to try to predict the scenario well in advance of any such pressure points and proactively try to drive through the budget increase request.

6. Settlement dynamics in funded cases

The dynamics between clients and funders when it comes to settlement discussions are variable. Where the merits of a case have changed, either the client or funder may wish to settle for a modest sum; whereas the other party may wish to carry on, hoping to secure a higher recovery. If they perceive a serious risk to achieving a favourable return for their investors, some funders may threaten to withdraw funding (subject to the terms of the funding agreement) or refuse to agree a required budget variation in order to pressure clients to accept or make an offer to settle.

The topic of settlement should be proactively addressed at the most strategically optimal time. If it is too early, the client may fear that it will convey weakness to the opponent; but the later it is left, the more money will have been committed. The stakes are then higher and tensions increase.

Be prepared to discuss 'early' settlements with clients. An early settlement offer may appear to be less than what the client expects, but by settling on the steps of the court, proportionately more will be paid away to the funder. Funders are more likely to be flexible (eg, discounting the multiple) on an earlier settlement. However, once you get close to trial, the funder may take a harder line, having already been exposed to funding the trial costs.

Top tips for bringing clients, funders and insurers through settlement discussions and to an acceptable outcome for all include the following:

- If possible, pre-agree with stakeholders acceptable parameters for settlement, thereby making negotiations as efficient as possible.
- Ensure that all stakeholders have representatives who are readily contactable at the time of the settlement discussions so that decisions can be made quickly.
- At any settlement meeting or mediation, bring outcomes modelling/spreadsheets where figures can be inputted easily to enable you to have an informed debate with other stakeholders about differing offers and the net result for all.
- Manage client expectations from the outset and help the client to make commercially savvy decisions.

7. Disputes relating to funded cases

The main sources of disputes with funders are:

- budget overage;
- when and at what amount to settle the case; and
- the shares of proceeds recovered.

These disputes can be a point of tension in the lawyer/client relationship. In some cases, some funders seek to dominate the relationship with clients and blame the instructed lawyers for difficult issues that have arisen, even when these are a by-product of the actions of the opponent or the tribunal. The best way for law firms to mitigate this risk is to keep their funded clients informed and involved in issues arising with the funder.

Top tips for managing the risk of funder disputes include the following:

- Ensure good engagement with the funder at the start to minimise the risk of disputes later. Remember, funder disputes are a big drain of time.
- Keep the client fully apprised and on board at all times. All steps below must be discussed with the client to avoid them becoming a nasty surprise.
- Propose mediation to the funder where appropriate.
- If the funding dispute becomes protracted, consider lining up other funders or other forms of alternative funding agreements and, in a non-aggressive manner, put these to the funder. Showing that your client has both an alternative and a willingness to invoke an assessment or termination can be effective in bringing obstinate funders around.
- In extreme situations, lawyers may have to contemplate invoking a 'pens down' scenario. However, this must be strategically planned and scheduled, avoiding any key hearings or steps in the case.

Most litigation funding agreements will contain express clauses that govern dispute resolution. It is important to check and follow those terms, in relation to both notification to commence a dispute and the forum for its resolution. Often, this will involve either expert determination or arbitration, with driving factors being:

- speed;
- confidentiality;
- finality; and
- having an appointed expert or arbitrator with significant experience in cost and funding issues.

Some disputes may involve the instructed law firm and/or insurer. Ideally, that scenario will have been foreseen at the outset so that all related alternative funding agreements provide for the same dispute resolution process.

Other common types of cost and funding disputes can include:

- disputes between the client, funder, ATE insurers and/or law firm over the shares of proceeds recovered under the priorities agreement;
- *inter partes* costs assessments;

- solicitor and client cost assessments (including where allegations of unenforceable fee agreements such as a CFA are raised);
- cost-sharing disputes in multi-party or group claims;
- professional negligence claims relating to a lack of advice on, or suitability of, alternative funding arrangements or ATE insurance;
- post-*PACCAR*[1] litigation funding agreement enforceability disputes; and
- insurance coverage or legal expense payment disputes relating to ATE, professional indemnity insurance and directors' and officers' insurance policies.

It may be necessary or advisable for the parties to cost and funding disputes to be independently represented, as conflicts of interest may arise between:

- the client and the law firm it instructed; or
- the funder and the law firm that drafted the funding agreement for it.

Notes

1 *R (on the application of PACCAR Inc) v Competition Appeal Tribunal* [2023] UKSC 28.

About the authors

Matthew Amey
Director, TheJudge
matthew.amey@thejudgeglobal.com

Matthew Amey has been a director of TheJudge since 2005, having previously worked as an underwriter for a market-leading litigation insurer. Since then, TheJudge has expanded in the United States, Canada and continental Europe; and Matthew's role in the market has been recognised by industry peers after he was included in the *Chambers & Partners Litigation Funding Brokers* rankings for four years in a row.

Matthew has been at the cutting edge of developments in litigation-related insurance and finance for over two decades and has placed some of the largest, most complex one-off litigation insurance policies in existence. They include judgment preservation insurance, damages-based agreement (DBA)/contingency fee insurance and arbitration award default cover.

In January 2021, Matthew, along with his co-founders, launched a new litigation funder called Erso Capital to complement TheJudge's insurance broker services.

Craig Arnott
Deputy chief investment officer, Burford Capital
carnott@burfordcapital.com

Craig Arnott is deputy chief investment officer with specific responsibility for Burford's investment portfolio in the United Kingdom, the European Union, the Middle East and Australasia. Craig is a member of Burford's management and investment committees. Prior to joining Burford, Craig advised the company while serving as barrister at Sixth Floor Selborne and Wentworth Chambers in Sydney. Before being called to the Bar, he was a partner and head of competition law in London at international firm Fried Frank. He commenced his career at Cravath, Swaine & Moore in New York.

Stavros Brekoulakis
Michael and Laura Hwang Chair of International Arbitration, National University of Singapore; Arbitrator, 3 Verulam Buildings
sbrekoulakis@3vb.com

Stavros Brekoulakis is the Michael and Laura Hwang Chair of International Arbitration at the National University of Singapore. Stavros also practises as an arbitrator at 3 Verulam Buildings (Gray's Inn). He is the author of eight monographs, books and edited volumes and more than 30 articles in leading peer-reviewed law journals.

Stavros has led important policy projects and advised governmental, intergovernmental and non-governmental organisations, including as the co-chair of the International Council for Commercial Arbitration (ICCA)-Queen Mary University London (QMUL) Task Force on Third Party Funding and a member of the London Bar Reform Committee. He is currently a member of the governing body of ICCA; the Governing Court of the London Court of International Arbitration (LCIA); and the International Chamber of Commerce (ICC) Commission on Arbitration.

He is the editor-in-chief of the *International Journal of Arbitration, Mediation and Dispute Management*; the general editor of the *Journal of International Dispute Settlement*; the co-editor of Kluwer's International Arbitration Law Library Series; and a member of the editorial board of *Arbitration International.*

Julian Chamberlayne
Risk and funding partner, Stewarts
jchamberlayne@stewartslaw.com

Julian Chamberlayne is the risk and funding partner at Stewarts. His role involves developing and implementing improvements to the legal services that Stewarts provides to all of its clients, including innovative cost and funding options such as the Stewarts Litigate insurance facility. He chairs the firm's risk and funding committee, which proactively reviews issues relating to clients, cases and/or applications that involve financial, reputational or regulatory risks, including approving and monitoring alternative funding arrangements for major commercial dispute cases. He also leads Stewarts' cost and funding disputes team.

For over two decades, Julian has been instrumental in making Stewarts a leader in the field of costs and funding in the United Kingdom. Stewarts was an early adopter of conditional fee agreements, damages-based agreements, after-the-event insurance and third-party litigation funding. Julian has also played a prominent role in campaigning for law reform in relation to cost and funding issues to enhance options for Stewarts' clients.

Moeiz Farhan
Barrister, 36 Stone
mfarhan@36stone.co.uk

Moeiz Farhan has a broad commercial practice and has extensive experience of international commercial litigation and arbitration. Before joining 36 Stone, he worked for several years as an employed barrister in the world-leading disputes practices of Gibson Dunn and King & Spalding. His work at those firms included advising and acting on behalf of some of the world's largest and most well-known companies, often on high-value and high-profile matters. His experience working at large international law firms means that he is equally comfortable working independently or as part of a team.

Before coming to the Bar, Moeiz was a research assistant at the Law Commission of England and Wales, where he worked on the Law Commission's review of the law of fiduciary duties and its application to investment intermediaries. The Law Commission's report, which he was heavily involved in drafting, has been cited by the courts at all levels, including by the Supreme Court in *R (on the application of Palestine Solidarity Campaign Ltd and another) v Secretary of State for Housing, Communities and Local Government* [2020] 1 WLR 1774. He was also a visiting tutor at King's College London.

Steven Friel
Chief executive officer, Woodsford
sfriel@woodsford.com

Steven Friel is CEO at Woodsford, a leading collective redress business. An English solicitor, Steven is an *alumnus* of Cambridge

University and the Inns of Court School of Law, and graduated top of his class with a master of laws in international dispute resolution from the University of London. He has been listed as a leader in litigation finance in every annual ranking by *Chambers & Partners*, *The Legal 500*, *Lawdragon Global* and *Who's Who Legal*. He was named as one of the PwC Top 10 Inspirational Leaders 2020 in the British LGBT Awards; and one of the Top 100 Gamechangers 2022, in partnership with Citi, as a leader in diversity, equity and inclusion across the global financial services industry. He is the managing editor of leading treatise *The Law and Business of Litigation Finance* (Bloomsbury Professional); a member of the advisory board at the Centre for Sustainable Governance and Law in the Built Environment at University College London; and a member of the Global Stewardship Committee of the International Corporate Governance Network.

Ewelina Kajkowska
Senior associate, Hogan Lovells International LLP
ewelina.kajkowska@hoganlovells.com

Ewelina Kajkowska is a dispute resolution lawyer based in London. She focuses on international arbitration and has experience dealing with disputes under the LCIA, ICC, International Centre for Settlement of Investment Disputes (ICSID) and United Nations Commission on International Trade Law (UNCITRAL) rules. Ewelina also advises on alternative dispute resolution (ADR) methods and issues of jurisdiction and conflicts of law in international disputes.

Ewelina has practised across multiple jurisdictions. Prior to joining Hogan Lovells, she was an adviser to the Polish government in arbitration cases. She has also worked for a global law firm in the Middle East, advising clients on a range of matters before the Dubai International Financial Centre courts and arbitral tribunals.

Ewelina has extensive academic experience, having completed her PhD and post-doctoral research in international arbitration and ADR, and is a published author and speaker in the field.

David J Kerstein
Founder and managing director, Arcadia Finance LLC
dave@arcadiafin.com

David J Kerstein is the founder and managing director of Arcadia Finance, a commercial litigation finance company based in New York. Prior to founding Arcadia, Dave was one of the co-founders and managing directors of Validity Finance, where he co-led origination, underwriting, structuring and monitoring of investment opportunities. An early adopter of litigation finance with 10 years in the industry,

Dave serves as a trusted and strategic partner and adviser to lawyers and clients seeking to manage litigation risk and spend. Dave began his career in litigation finance at Bentham IMF, now Omni Bridgeway, where he spent four years as an investment manager. Before that, he spent 15 years as a trial lawyer handling complex commercial disputes at a leading international law firm, Gibson Dunn.

Dave is a sought-after speaker and recognised leader in litigation finance. He has been named among *Lawdragon*'s "Global 100 Leaders in Legal Finance" and selected by *Who's Who Legal* as a "Thought Leader in Third Party Funding".

Julian DM Lew KC
Arbitrator, Twenty Essex; Head of the School of International Arbitration, Queen Mary University of London
jlew@twentyessex.com

Julian DM Lew KC is a full-time arbitrator in international commercial and investment disputes at Twenty Essex. He has been involved in international arbitration for more than 40 years as an academic, counsel and arbitrator. He has been appointed and has conducted arbitrations under the rules of all the major arbitral institutions and under the UNCITRAL Arbitration Rules. Julian has been professor and head of the School of International Arbitration, QMUL since its creation in 1985. He has published extensively on international arbitration and has sat on the board of directors, management and advisory boards and research committees of several major international arbitration institutions. Julian established and is the co-editor of Kluwer's International Arbitration Law Library Series.

Matthew Lo
Director, Exton Advisors
matthew.lo@extonadvisors.com

Matthew Lo is an English law-qualified, former private practice disputes lawyer with a wealth of experience in litigation funding. Having trained and practised at global business law firm DLA Piper since 2015, he has a strong background in international dispute resolution, with a particular focus on complex and cross-border commercial, corporate, energy and natural resources and fraud disputes. Since switching to a career in litigation funding with Aldersgate Funding in 2020 and subsequently with Exton Advisors from 2023, Matt has covered every aspect of the funding process, from origination to execution. Matt's skill set includes legal and financial due diligence, bespoke advisory work, price modelling and structuring of litigation funding and legal risk insurance arrangements.

Sherina Petit
Partner and head of international arbitration and India practice, Stewarts
spetit@stewartslaw.com

Sherina Petit is the head of the international arbitration department at Stewarts and head of the India practice. She also sits on the executive board of the firm. Sherina specialises in international commercial arbitration, investor-state arbitration, litigation and ADR. In addition to acting as counsel in arbitration, she sits as an arbitrator. Sherina is ranked in all the major directories, including the *Legal Business* Arbitration Power List, and as a Global Leader in *Who's Who Legal*. Sherina has achieved a number of successes for her clients in both commercial and investment arbitration proceedings in terms of settlement and arbitration awards. She has a wide range of experience in all key aspects of international arbitration, including under all the major arbitral institution rules, with a focus on India-related disputes. Her global client base spans a broad range of industries, including energy, construction, oil and gas, trade, transport, pharmaceuticals, commodities, finance and technology.

Michael Redman
Co-head of Europe, Middle East and Africa, Burford Capital
mredman@burfordcapital.com

Michael Redman is a co-head of Europe, Middle East and Africa and head of the London office, with responsibility for the business generated and managed out of the United Kingdom and Europe. Michael continues to be deeply involved in asset recovery and contentious insolvency matters in particular, while also overseeing origination and underwriting across the region. Michael is a leading authority on enforcement finance and complex asset recovery, with almost two decades of experience in the field.

A trained barrister, Michael began his career in the Lloyd's of London political and credit risk insurance market and also spent time in the West African diamond industry. He has worked in complex asset recovery and enforcement for close to two decades, holding senior private sector positions in both Moscow and London before co-founding a leading asset recovery advisory boutique.

Vasanti Selvaratnam KC
Senior silk and joint head of chambers (2018–2023), 36 Stone
vselvaratnam@36stone.co.uk; vasantiselvaratnam@gmail.com

Vasanti Selvaratnam KC is a senior silk and former joint head of chambers at 36 Stone. She divides her time between sitting as an international independent commercial arbitrator in disputes covering a wide range of industries under all the major institutional rules and appearing as an advocate in high-profile commercial cases. She has been recognised in *All About Shipping* as one of the top 24 remarkable women who have substantially contributed to the international maritime industry; and was shortlisted for *Chambers UK* Bar Awards Shipping Silk of the Year 2022.

Vasanti appeared in the leading funding case *Arkin v Borchard Lines*, which capped the funder's liability to the level of the investment. She has also written on the topic of good faith under English law and recently contributed to the work of the Financial Markets Law Committee on duties of good faith in wholesale financial contracts.

Nicole Silver
Lead underwriter and head of US operations, Ignite Specialty Risk
nicole.silver@ignitespecialty.com

Nicole Silver is the lead underwriter and head of US operations at Ignite Specialty Risk, a managing general agent specialising in capital protection insurance. Prior to getting into the insurance space, Nicole served as an investment manager at Validity Finance, one of the premier litigation funders operating in the United States. In addition, Nicole has a 20-year track record of success litigating complex disputes. She has worked at Winston & Strawn and was a partner at Greenberg Traurig. She has appeared before numerous courts and tribunals, including the US Supreme Court, various appellate and district courts, the ICDR, ICC, ICSID, UNCITRAL and the USTR.

Nicole has been named one of Latin America's Top 100 Female Lawyers by Latinvex, 2016–2021; and was recognised in *Latin Lawyer*'s Latin Lawyer 250 – Practice Recognition: Arbitration in 2020. She was also recognised in *Global Arbitration Review*'s Who's Who Future Leaders in 2022 and the GAR 100 Survey in 2018; and earned inclusion in *The Legal 500 US* in 2018. Nicole is a graduate of Vanderbilt Law School and received her BA from Princeton University.

Nishant Nath Singh
Senior associate, Stewarts
nsingh@stewartslaw.com

Nishant Nath Singh is a disputes lawyer at Stewarts. He specialises in international arbitration and commercial litigation. Nishant's experience covers arbitration proceedings under the major institutional rules, and he regularly advises clients on large and complex litigation matters before the English courts (some of which have involved third-party funding). Nishant also works within Stewarts'

India practice and has a wide-ranging and varied experience in advising clients on India-focused matters.

Before joining Stewarts, Nishant worked at Slaughter and May on commercial litigation, international arbitration and investigation matters. He trained at Norton Rose Fulbright. Nishant is originally from New Delhi, India and moved to the United Kingdom to study law and business at the University of Warwick.

Mick Smith
Principal, Burford Capital
micksmith@burfordcapital.com

Mick Smith is a principal with responsibility for leading Burford's investment activity and operations in Europe, focusing on companies, funds, investors and law firms engaged in commercial litigation and arbitration. Mick co-founded Calunius Capital. He previously practised law at Freshfields in both London and Madrid, and then worked as an investment banker at JPMorgan Chase, Credit Agricole Lazard and Dresdner Kleinwort.

Tom Steindler
Managing director, Exton Advisors
tom.steindler@extonadvisors.com

Tom Steindler has nearly a decade of experience in the financing of disputes and other legal assets, as well as corporate finance and litigation risk insurance. He is a recognised thought leader in litigation funding and has led a wide range of transactions, from the financing of single claims, portfolios and law firms to the monetisation of awards. Tom holds a master's in finance from King's Business School.

Hasan Tahsin Azizagaoglu
Associate, Bench Walk Advisors
hasan.tahsin@benchwalk.com

Hasan Tahsin Azizagaoglu works at Bench Walk Advisors, where he oversees the due diligence process for proposed cases for funding, the negotiation of funding arrangements and the subsequent management of cases. He has been recognised by several directories, including *Lawdragon*, and named among the 2023 and 2024 *Lawdragon* 100 Global Leaders in Litigation Finance. Additionally, he serves as the co-chair of the third-party funding group at the Chartered Institute of Arbitrators and is a member of the organising committee for Istanbul Arbitration Days. He holds a PhD in private international law.

Harshiv Thakerar
Chief investment officer, Asertis
harshiv.thakerar@asertis.co.uk

Harshiv Thakerar has more than six years' experience in litigation funding and has been responsible for successful investments and resolutions across a breadth of claims in the industry. Prior to joining Asertis, Harshiv headed the litigation funding division at Global Growth Cap and, prior to that, was head of commercial litigation at Augusta Ventures. He qualified as a litigation solicitor at Mishcon de Reya and has founded and invested in business in the real estate and tech sectors.

Praised for his "pragmatism and hands-on approach", Harshiv is ranked in *Chambers* for Litigation Funding. *Chambers* also notes that Harshiv "acts on solid mandates including enforcement actions, competition claims and group action cases".

Harshiv holds an LLB (Hons) and is a practising solicitor in England.

Nosherwan Vakil
The 36 Group
nvakil@36group.co.uk

Nosherwan Vakil has been practising as a lawyer for over 15 years in India. He is also a barrister of England and Wales. He acts as counsel before various courts in India, including the Supreme Court of India, High Courts and Tribunals. Nosherwan's practice focuses on commercial disputes in international arbitrations and in Indian courts.

Nosherwan is a door tenant with a leading English chamber, The 36 Group, in London, consisting of international barristers, mediators and arbitrators.

Simona Valkova
Independent tribunal secretary
simona.iv.valkova@gmail.com

Simona Valkova is an independent tribunal secretary specialising in international commercial and investment arbitration. She has been working in the international arbitration field for over five years and has experience with arbitrations under a variety of institutional and *ad hoc* rules (eg, ICC, Hong Kong International Arbitration Centre, LCIA, Singapore International Arbitration Centre, Stockholm Chamber of Commerce, ICSID and UNCITRAL Rules). She is qualified to practise law as a solicitor in England and Wales. Simona is also a teaching fellow in international commercial and investment arbitration law at the School of International Arbitration, QMUL.

Ayse Yazir
Global head of origination, Bench Walk Advisors
ayse@benchwalk.com

Ayse Yazir is the global head of origination and has an outstanding reputation in the litigation funding industry, where she originates, underwrites and monitors funding in various litigation sectors, including international and commercial arbitration, insolvency, class actions and global litigation matters. Prior to joining Bench Walk Advisors, Ayse worked at Gallagher's and she has seven years' senior technical underwriting experience with a global funder. Ayse has been instrumental in drafting rules on third-party funding for both UNCITRAL and ICSID and is currently working at the Chartered Institute of Arbitrators' Third-Party Funding drafting committee.

She has been recognised as a "Thought Leader: Third-Party Funding" by *Who's Who Legal* for four consecutive years; ranked in *Chambers & Partners* in both the United Kingdom and Europe; named in *The Legal 500* as an industry leader; named as one of the top 10 most influential litigation funders by *Business Today*; and ranked by *Lawdragon* as a leading funder. Ayse won "Leading Dispute Resolution Expert" at the *Lawyer Monthly* Awards 2020, 2021, 2022 and 2023; and won the "Litigation Funder of the Year" award at the *Finance Monthly* Awards 2021 and 2023.

About Globe Law and Business

Globe Law and Business was established in 2005. From the very beginning, we set out to create legal books that are sufficiently high level to be of real use to the experienced professional, yet still accessible and easy to navigate. Most of our authors are drawn from Magic Circle and other top commercial firms, both in the United Kingdom and internationally.

Our titles are carefully produced, with the utmost attention paid to editorial, design and production processes. We hope this results in high-quality publications that are easy to read and a pleasure to own.

In 2021, we were very pleased to announce the start of a new chapter for Globe Law and Business following the acquisition of law books under the imprint Ark Publishing. Our law firm management list is now significantly expanded with many well-known and loved Ark Publishing titles.

We are also pleased to announce the launch of our online content platform, Globe Law Online, which allows for easy search and networked access across firms. Details of all titles included can be found at www.globelawonline.com. Email glo@globelawandbusiness.com for further details and to arrange a free trial for you or your firm.

We'd very much like to hear from you with your thoughts and ideas for improving what we offer. Please do feel free to email me on sian@globelawandbusiness.com. Happy reading and thank you for your time.

Sian O'Neill
Managing director
Globe Law and Business
www.globelawandbusiness.com